# History,
# Law and
# Christianity

JOHN WARWICK MONTGOMERY is considered by many to be the foremost living apologist for biblical Christianity. A renaissance scholar with a flair for controversy, he lives in France, England and the United States. His international activities have brought him into personal contact with some of the most exciting events of our time; not only was he in China in June 1989, but he was in Fiji during its 1987 bloodless revolution, was involved in assisting East Germans to escape during the time of the Berlin Wall, and was in Paris during the "days of May" 1968.

Dr. Montgomery is the author of more than sixty books in six languages. He holds eleven earned degrees, including a Master of Philosophy in Law from the University of Essex, England, an LL.M. and the earned higher doctorate in law (LL.D.) from Cardiff University, Wales, a Ph.D. from the University of Chicago, and a Doctorate of the University in Protestant Theology from the University of Strasbourg, France. He is an ordained Lutheran clergyman, an English barrister, a French *avocat* (Paris bar), and is admitted to practice as a lawyer before the Supreme Court of the United States. He obtained acquittals for the "Athens 3" missionaries on charges of proselytism at the Greek Court of Appeals in 1986, and has won four religious cases at the European Court of Human Rights.

Dr. Montgomery is Professor Emeritus of Law and Humanities, University of Bedfordshire, England, and Distinguished Research Professor of Philosophy, Concordia University Wisconsin, U.S.A. He is listed in *Who's Who in America*, *Who's Who in France*, *Who's Who in Europe*, and *Who's Who in the World*.

Dr. Montgomery has written and lectured extensively on the evidences for the truth of Christianity. A list of his related books and audio recordings will be found in the "Suggestions for Further Study" at the end of this book. These materials are available at www.1517legacy.com.

# History,
# Law and
# Christianity

With a commendatory letter from C.S. Lewis

John Warwick Montgomery,
Ph.D., LL.D., Th.D.

*History, Law, and Christianity*

Published by:
NRP Books, an imprint of 1517. The Legacy Project
PO Box 54032
Irvine, CA 92619-4032

Printed in the United States of America

Library of Congress Cataloging-in-Publication Data

Library of Congress Control Number: 2015938178

ISBN 978-1-945500-01-5

NRP Books is committed to packaging and promoting the finest content for fueling a new Lutheran Reformation. We promote the defense of the Christian faith, confessional Lutheran theology, vocation and civil courage.

*For*

## Howard, Jane, & Sara Hoffman

*and*

## George Poulos

*"Maecenas atavis edite regibus,*
*O et praesidium et dulce decus meum . . ."*

(Horace, *Odes*, I, 1)

# Contents

# Foreword

Author of more than 60 books in 6 languages and with 11 earned degrees in history, law, theology, and philosophy (including three earned doctorates), John Warwick Montgomery has been on the intellectual forefront of the defense of the claims of Christianity for well over five decades. While historians and lawyers have in fact long been some of Christianity's strongest proponents, rarely have the benefits of both of these disciplines been so effectively presented in making the case for the facticity of Christian truth claims as is done in this brilliant volume.

The "historical evidences" section is probably the best-known of Montgomery's works and has a fascinating genesis in a series of public lectures presented by him at the University of British Columbia, Canada over a generation ago. These lectures came in response to philosophy professor Avrum Stroll's controversial claim at the time (rehashed now by such contemporary critics as Bart Ehrman) that knowledge of the historical Jesus was shrouded in hopeless mystery resulting from centuries of textual corruption of the New Testament records. At one particularly awkward moment, Stroll was reminded by Montgomery in public repartee that rejection of the textual tradition supporting the New Testament picture of Jesus Christ meant the loss of certainty about **all** of classical history. Though now with the barbed hook firmly inserted in his mouth, Stroll remained undaunted and fired back: "Fine, I will throw out my knowledge of the classical world." At that stunning admission, the then Chairman of the Classics Department leapt up and shrieked, "Good Lord Avrum, not that!"

This only goes to show that one rejects the central argument of this volume at one's intellectual, indeed in some cases even academic, peril.

There is a good reason why this work has gone through multiple editions in five translations and why the manuscript in its infancy received the highest of accolades from no less a weighty authority than C.S. Lewis (see below for the correspondence Montgomery received from Lewis as a result of a request that Lewis consider coming to UBC to lecture). This classic uniquely combines both *historical* and *legal* evidences in order to render a verdict for the accuracy of the biblical picture of Jesus Christ based on what we in trial law call evidence that is "beyond a reasonable doubt."

In the first section on historical evidences, Montgomery sets forth a trio of tests to determine the reliability of the New Testament Gospels. The case for the essential historicity of the Gospel narratives is found to rest on the rich textual tradition that buttresses the New Testament in general and the Gospel records in particular. Matthew, Mark, Luke and John, as a result of the strict application of the canons of textual criticism, turn out to be the best attested works of the ancient world. Montgomery arrives at this conclusion not by employing "theological" or "faith based" criteria unacceptable in classical studies, but by rigorously applying the widely-accepted scholarly standards used by anyone seeking to determine the authenticity of any text of classical antiquity.

The second section of the book deals with "legal evidences" and is built upon the author's professional standing as an English barrister, French *avocat*, and American attorney. It, too, has an interesting pedigree, with much of the material originally presented by Montgomery as part of his invitational lecture at the Victoria Institute (the Philosophical Society of Great Britain), founded in 1865 by the Earl of Shaftesbury, and whose past presidents have included Sir Frederic Kenyon, Professor F.F. Bruce, and Sir Norman Anderson. Here Montgomery sets forth the case for Christianity using the evidential standards derived from the common law, where presuppositions are kept to the bare minimum. The least amount of data is assumed (only presuppositions of form, such as assuming the objectivity of the external world, the inferential operations of induction and deduction, the meaningfulness of language, and the validity of the law of non-contradiction) so that the maximum amount of data is capable of being discovered.

The import of Montgomery's juridical approach (developed in depth in other works of his such as *Christ Our Advocate* and *Human*

*Rights and Human Dignity*) is seen in at least three very practical areas: First, is the concept of probability reasoning; second, is his use of the principle of the "burden of proof;" and finally is his insistence that a *verdict* be rendered on that evidence.

First, with respect to probability reasoning, Montgomery presents the position that the case for Christianity is ultimately a case based on establishing the facticity of certain events (as opposed to arguing that Christianity is true because it is necessarily the most "logical" system). *If certain events did not occur, Christianity is a sham. Period.* Facts never rise to the level of formal, mathematical proof. Thus, the case for Christianity is never apodictically certain because 100 percent certainty only comes in matters of deductive logic or pure mathematics. One weighs probabilities, looks at the facts as a lawyer would in presenting evidence to a court or jury, and then a decision must be rendered. One must never demand of religious claims a level of factual certainty not demanded in any other domain.

Second, Montgomery stresses that the "burden of proof" is actually on the Christian to establish the case for Christianity. This has direct practical implications. Christians will see the importance of bringing the case for Christ into the marketplace and stressing arguments that can be checked out. This emphasis on the Christian assuming the burden of proof means that legal apologetics is more interested in focusing on *positive*, fact-driven arguments for the case for Christianity than it is in tearing down the weaker arguments of other world religions or philosophies.

Third, as a skilled trial lawyer, Montgomery knows that as a plaintiff with the burden of proof, the key is the return of a favorable verdict. The law recognizes this fact since even an executive pardon must be "accepted" to be effective. The mere acceptance of facts, though, is not enough when confronted with the claims of Christianity. If the factual case is sound—as a legion of trial lawyers have concluded for centuries that it is, owing to the overwhelmingly solid evidence in its favor—then personal commitment to the central figure revealed in those same facts is both reasonable and required.

This book presents a unique and seamless integration of evidences derived from both historical and legal methodologies, producing a case of staggering consequence for the serious inquirer. Having survived and thrived almost five decades of analysis and critique, this work stands as Montgomery's best known—and for good reason. Another generation of readers can now continue to benefit from it.

Craig A. Parton
On the Feast of Doubting Thomas
Santa Barbara, California
December 21, 2014

**CRAIG PARTON** is a trial attorney and partner with a Santa Barbara law firm—the oldest law firm west of Mississippi River—and is the United States Director of the International Academy of Apologetics, Evangelism and Human Rights in Strasbourg, France. Dr. Montgomery is Director of that Academy, which takes place in Strasbourg, France, each July (www.apologeticsacademy.eu)

# Introduction

This book has an interesting history.

The first part (the "historical" section) began its life as a series of lectures at the University of British Columbia, Canada, in response to a widely publicized address by a philosophy professor who claimed that our historical knowledge of Jesus Christ was woefully inadequate. When I argued that so good was the historical picture of Jesus that, to eliminate it, one would have—literally—to throw out one's knowledge of the classical world in general, Professor Avrum Stroll replied, "Fine: I shall throw out my knowledge of the classical world." Whereupon, the then chairman of the U.B.C. Classics Department jumped up crying, "Good Lord, Avrum, not that!"

Mimeographed copies of my lectures circulated in Canada for some time. They then became a series of four articles in the old *His* magazine published by the Inter-Varsity Christian Fellowship (December 1964 to March 1965). Subsequently the articles were published and distributed as a *His* reprint, and this led to their issuance in book form by Inter-Varsity Press. In 1983, Here's Life Publishers, the publishing arm of Campus Crusade for Christ, took the book over; and from there it went to Bethany House Publishers, where its production run reached some 20,000 copies. The book has been translated into French, German, Spanish and Chinese, and has been widely read in Europe, Central and South America, and the Far East.

There is an interesting aftermath to the presentation of the original lectures. Since I was already corresponding with C.S. Lewis, the Lutheran Student Movement of Canada asked me to invite Lewis to lecture at U.B.C., further to develop the apologetic issues that had been raised in the Stroll-Montgomery debate. The following reply was one of the last letters Lewis wrote before his death less than three months later (22 November 1963). This letter has not appeared in any collection of Lewis' correspondence:

Oxford 29 August '63

Dear Mr. Montgomery,

I am afraid the days of my lecturing and traveling are over. Last July my death was hourly expected, and tho' I didn't get through the gate I have had to resign all my posts and settle down (not unhappily) to the life of an invalid.

Your two lectures did me good and I shall constantly find them useful. Congratulations. The only criticism I'd venture is that you have possibly a little bit over-called the blow about *kyrios*. Admittedly, like Lat. *dominus* and English Lord, it may represent JHVH: but like them it can also mean a human superior. The vocative *kyrie* often needs to be translated "Sir" rather than "Lord." Otherwise I don't think it could be bettered.

Yours sincerely,<br>C.S. Lewis

The "law" part of the present volume first constituted a chapter in my comprehensive treatment of human rights—Human Rights and Human Dignity. The logic is that, if the only possible foundation for human rights is transcendental and revelational (as I show), it is imperative to demonstrate evidentially that God did in fact reveal himself in the human sphere. That legal argument then became an appropriate inclusion in the volume arising from the "Cornell Symposium on Christian Apologetics," which I was asked to edit (*Evidence for Faith: Deciding the God Question*). In 1998, the same material constituted my invitational lecture at the Victoria Institute (the Philosophical Society of Great Britain), founded in 1865 by the Earl of Shaftesbury, whose past presidents have included Sir Frederic Kenyon, Professor F.F. Bruce, and Sir Norman Anderson. The October 1998 number of the Institute's bulletin (*Faith & Thought*) was devoted entirely to its publication as a journal article.

What is the logic of cementing these two publications together in a single volume? The answer is, simply, that they represent complementary ways of investigating the critical question of Jesus' historicity. Both historical scholarship and legal proof center on evidence. Responsible historians and lawyers would agree entirely with Sherlock Holmes, who declared: "It is a capital mistake to theorize in advance of the facts." Here, we present the primary, relevant, "admissible" facts concerning the most influential single individual in the history of mankind. It is then up to the reader to give a personal answer to the question he posed to his contemporaries: "Who do you say that I am?"

A concluding prefatory word should perhaps be added for those who would discard this book *ab initio* because it does not appear to take any account of Postmodernist thinking. If Derrida and company are correct that there is no satisfactory objective knowledge of the world, its events and its writings—that noone can go beyond telling his or her "story" or be able to refute anyone else's—then quite obviously a book such as this (both parts of it) is hopelessly wide of the mark. The problem, however, lies not with this book, which employs methodologies fundamental to all scientific, historical and legal scholarship. The difficulty lies rather with the relativistic, solipsistic assumptions of Postmodernism in all its varieties. If objective knowledge is unattainable, then the knife must cut both ways: there will be no way to show that Postmodernist theory is itself preferable to contradictory ideologies! And if the Postmodernist were correct, no practical knowledge, based on experience and evidence, would be possible. Each individual would become, in effect, one of Leibniz's monads, living in his or her own special universe and incapable of understanding any other. No one in reality ever lives this way. Each and every one of us must assume the reliability of our evidential examinations of the world in order to live in it. This book asks only that the reader be honest enough with himself or herself to apply those very same, essential techniques of investigation to the most important question one can possibly raise, namely, was Jesus correct or not when he declared: "I am the way, and the truth, and the life; no one comes to the Father but by me"? (John 14:6)

John Warwick Montgomery
Christmas Day, A.D. 2001

# Historical Evidence

# Who Is Jesus Christ?

The earliest records we have of the life and ministry of Jesus give the overwhelming impression that this man went around not so much "doing good" as making a decided nuisance of himself.

The parallel with Socrates in this regard is strong: both men infuriated their contemporaries to such an extent that they were eventually put to death. But where Socrates played the gadfly on the collective Athenian rump by demanding that his hearers "know themselves"—examine their unexamined lives—Jesus alienated his contemporaries by continually forcing them to think through their attitude to him personally. "Who do men say that I the Son of man am?" "Who do you say that I am?" "What do you think of Christ? Whose son is he?" These were the questions Jesus asked. And it seems patently clear that the questioner was not asking because he really didn't know who Jesus was and needed help in finding out! Unlike the "sick" characters in Jules Feiffer's Greenwich Village cartoons, when Jesus asked, "Who am I?" he was evidently fully aware of his own character. What he sought to achieve by his questions was a similar awareness of his nature by others.

In these chapters I shall again pose Jesus' irritating questions concerning himself: Who was he? Who did he claim to be? Is there compelling evidence in support of these claims? The next two chapters will discuss the documentary basis of Jesus' life and claims, and thereby provide the necessary background for the last two chapters in which the claims themselves will be explicitly set forth, together with the attestation for them by way of the resurrection.

In spite of the tension which these issues will engender (they have always done so, since they inevitably require a rethinking of one's personal *Weltanschauung*—one's philosophy of life), I raise the questions with pleasure, since once upon a time, when I was an undergraduate philosophy student at Cornell University, I myself encountered this crucial problem-area, and as a result became a Christian believer. Like Cambridge professor C.S. Lewis, I was brought "kicking and struggling"[1] into the kingdom of God by the historical evidence in behalf of Jesus' claims. The resulting experiential (existential, if you will) satisfaction with the Christian worldview makes me more than willing to present the case for your consideration.

To get at the essential issue, I wish to recount a situation that developed at the University of British Columbia several years ago. Dr. Avrum Stroll of the Philosophy Department delivered a lecture titled, "Did Jesus Really Exist?"[2] Professor Stroll's remarks were widely publicized, and I replied to them in the public press. His position—which I regard as historically untenable—is summed up in the closing sentence of his address;

> An accretion of legends grew up about this figure [Jesus], was incorporated into the Gospels by various devotees of the movement, was rapidly spread throughout the Mediterranean world by the ministry of St. Paul; and that because this is so, it is impossible to separate these legendary elements in the purported descriptions of Jesus from those which in fact were true of him.

In my judgment, Professor Stroll arrives at this conclusion as a result of committing four serious historical-philosophical errors, and we shall take these up forthwith.

But first I wish to indicate that in one very important respect at least, Dr. Stroll and I are in full agreement over against President Briggs of the University Philosophy Club, who declared in a Canadian Press news dispatch following the Stroll lecture, "As a matter of fact we consider these topics, atheism and Jesus Christ, as not very important"—as compared, for example, with the question of "whether the earth's fuel is running out." I regard the issues raised by Dr. Stroll as of paramount significance. If even a fraction of the claims which Jesus made for himself, and which his followers made for him, are true, then the uncommitted will find themselves faced with what Paul Tillich has

---

[1] C.S. Lewis, *Surprised by Joy* (New York: Harcourt, Brace & World, 1955), p. 229

[2] Stroll's address appears as Appendix A, "Did Jesus Really Exist?"

well termed a "shaking of the foundations"—the necessity for a complete realignment of personal philosophy. On the other hand, if Jesus' claims are unfounded, then the Apostle Paul was absolutely correct when he wrote that if Christ is not risen from the dead, then we Christians are of all men most miserable (1 Corinthians 15:14–19).

Astute observers of our neurotic epoch seem to be more concerned about the running out of the spiritual rather than the natural fuel supply of the world. And the question of the historical validity of Jesus' claims bears directly upon this 21st century religious bankruptcy. In spite of our radically different viewpoints on the *de facto* validity of the historical portrait of Jesus presented in the New Testament documents, I believe that Dr. Stroll would heartily second me when I express agreement with the following statement by Millar Burrows of Yale, the foremost American expert on the Dead Sea Scrolls:

> There is a type of Christian faith . . . rather strongly represented today, [that] regards the affirmations of Christian faith as confessional statements which the individual accepts as a member of the believing community, and which are not dependent on reason or evidence. Those who hold this position will not admit that historical investigation can have anything to say about the uniqueness of Christ. They are often skeptical as to the possibility of knowing anything about the historical Jesus, and seem content to dispense with such knowledge. I cannot share this point of view. I am profoundly convinced that the historic revelation of God in Jesus of Nazareth must be the cornerstone of any faith that is really Christian. Any historical question about the real Jesus who lived in Palestine nineteen centuries ago is therefore fundamentally important.[3]

---

[3]Millar Burrows, *More Light on the Dead Sea Scrolls* (New York: Viking Press, 1958), p. 55.

# Four Historical-Philosophical Errors

Granted the "fundamental importance" of the question Professor Stroll raises, how correct is he in arguing concerning Jesus that "the information we have about him is a composite of fact and legend which cannot reliably be untangled"? Professor Stroll's argument involves four major fallacies, and these vitiate his entire presentation. Two of these fallacies are of an historical character, and two are of a philosophical-logical nature. Taken together, they destroy his argument not only in historical and philosophical respects, but also in the theological sphere, since Christian theology cannot be divorced from logic and history. Let it be noted that I am not criticizing Dr. Stroll as a theologian (he himself expressly stated in his lecture that he was "not a theologian"); but I am claiming that he overstepped scholarly bounds in making his historical judgments and that he commits philosophical blunders incongruous with his academic specialization.

What are Dr. Stroll's four errors? We shall mention them briefly now and come back to each in turn as our discussion proceeds.

## Modern Authorities

First, he relies almost exclusively upon the judgments of modern "authorities" in dealing with the question of the reliability of the New Testament documents. The proper scholarly procedure is, of course, to face the documentary problems directly, by way of the accepted canons of historical and literary method. Professor Stroll himself points up this type of logical fallacy when he writes in his popular manual, *Philosophy Made Simple*[4]: "It is not the prestige of an

---

[4]Avrum Stroll and Richard Popkin, *Philosophy Made Simple* (Garden City: Doubleday, 1956), p. 165.

authority which makes a statement true or false, but rather the citing of evidence either to confirm or [sic] disconfirm the statement." Moreover, the modern "authorities" cited by Professor Stroll are consistently of a particular kind. They represent a radical tradition of New Testament criticism which reflects 19th century rationalistic presuppositions (e.g., Albert Schweitzer), and which issues in the form-critical school (*formgeschichtliche Methode*) of Dibelius and Bultmann—an approach regarded as misleading and outmoded by much of recent biblical scholarship. For example—and this instance is typical—A.H. McNeile of Trinity College, Dublin, and C.S.C. Williams of Merton College, Oxford, in their *Introduction to the Study of the New Testament*[5], present seven thoroughly damning criticisms of the *Formgeschichte* approach. We shall take up some of these criticisms in Chapter Three. What we wish to stress at this point is Professor Stroll's apparent lack of awareness of such criticisms.

## Primary Documents

Second, Dr. Stroll commits the unpardonable historical sin of neglecting primary documents. The earliest records of Christianity we possess are not the Gospel accounts but the letters of Paul. Dr. Stroll dispenses with these in one paragraph of nine lines in his twenty-page paper, on the remarkable grounds that "all of them have at one time or other been challenged as genuine" and that "Paul never met Jesus." In point of fact, except for the so-called Pastoral Epistles and Ephesians, it would be next to impossible to find any competent present-day scholarship that denies the Pauline authorship of the corpus of letters purporting to have been written by him. And the fact that Paul had not himself been one of Jesus' original disciples is of minor significance when we remember that the author of one of the four Gospels (Luke) also wrote the Book of Acts, in which every effort is made to show that Paul's teachings about Jesus were accepted by the original apostles as fully consistent with their own remembrance of Jesus' message.

---

[5]A.H. McNeile and C.S.C. Williams, *Introduction to the Study of the New Testament* (2nd. Ed.; Oxford: Clarendon Press, 1955).

## Begging the Question

Third, Professor Stroll again violates his own philosophical canons by committing the logical error of *petitio principii*: "begging the question." In Stroll's *Philosophy Made Simple*, we read: "The Fallacy of Begging the Question . . . occurs when either the same statement is used both as a premise and [sic] a conclusion in an argument, or when one of the premises could not be known to be true unless the conclusion were first assumed to be true."

How does this circular argumentation operate in Professor Stroll's own discussion of Jesus' existence? He writes: "Even if there were reason to believe some of the material [in the Gospels] to express eyewitness accounts of Jesus' life, the accretion of legend, the description of miracles performed by Jesus, which exist in these writings make it difficult, if not impossible, to extract from them any reliable historical testimony about the events described." Here Dr. Stroll says that regardless of the question of eyewitness testimony, he rejects the authenticity of the Gospel accounts on the ground that they attribute miracles to Jesus. But how does one know whether miracles occurred in connection with Jesus' life unless he investigates the primary documents? Obviously Dr. Stroll is arguing in a circle and presupposing that miracles did not in fact occur in Jesus' life. As C.S. Lewis effectively points out in his work, *Miracles*, in the course of analyzing Hume's classic argument against miracles:

> Now of course we must agree with Hume that if there is absolutely "uniform experience" against miracles, if in other words they have never happened, why then they never have. Unfortunately, we know the experience against them to be uniform only if we know that all the reports of them are false. And we can know all the reports to be false only if we know already that miracles have never occurred. In fact, we are arguing in a circle.[6]

As we shall see in the next chapter, no historian can legitimately rule out documentary evidence simply on the ground that it records remarkable events. If the documents are sufficiently reliable, the

---

[6]C.S. Lewis, *Miracles* (New York: The Macmillan Company, 1947), p. 121–124.

remarkable events must be accepted even if they cannot be success-
fully explained by analogy with other events or by an *a priori* scheme
of natural causation. L.J. McGinley's criticism of Bultmann—upon
whom Dr. Stroll heavily relies—can as well be applied to him:
"Whenever Bultmann denies the historic worth of a passage because
of the supernatural content, he has ceased to be . . . an historian evaluating sources . . . and his criticisms have no value in the study of the
Gospel text."[7]

## Essene Messiahs

Last, Professor Stroll erroneously explains the "unhistorical" picture
of Jesus in the New Testament documents as the product of a "messianic fever" characteristic of the Palestinian Jews living under the
yoke of Roman oppression in the first century of our era. He parallels
the Essene "messiahs" of the Dead Sea Scrolls with Jesus, and argues
that the "psychological instability" of the time produced a divine
Christ out of an eschatologically-oriented Nazarene teacher by the
name of Jesus. As we shall see, this entire argument demonstrates
a baleful and inexcusable ignorance of the nature of Jewish messianic expectation at the time of Christ. Historically it can be proven
beyond question that, on every important point, Jesus' conception of
himself as Messiah differed radically from the conceptions held by
all parties among the Jews, and particularly that it cannot be harmo-
nized with the Essene "Teacher of Righteousness" described in the
scrolls from the Dead Sea. Moreover, as we shall also see, the trans-
formation of a human Jesus to a divine Christ was a task of which
neither the apostolic company nor Paul was psychologically or ethically capable—even if Jesus had met their stereotyped messianic
expectations, which he did not. Here Professor Stroll has stepped
onto quicksand where his unhistorical allegations are totally incapable of bearing philosophical weight.

---

[7]L.J. McGinley, *Form-Criticism of the Synoptic Healing Narratives* (Woodstock:
Woodstock College Press, 1944), p. 71.

# Are the New Testament Documents Historically Trustworthy?

So much for our rapid overview of the principal fallacies in Dr. Stroll's paper. Now we shall take the first of the major questions to be dealt with, namely, are the New Testament documents of sufficient historical worth that we can gain from them a reliable picture of Jesus' claims concerning himself and of the claims made for him by others? Here, let it be noted, we do not naively assume the "inspiration" or "infallibility" of the New Testament records, and then by circular reasoning attempt to prove what we have previously assumed. We will regard the documents (even though today they are usually printed on fine India paper with verse numbers) only as documents, and we will treat them as we would any other historical materials. Our procedure in determining documentary reliability will avoid Professor Stroll's first error—that of deferring to modern, rationalistic "authorities"—for we shall go directly to the documents themselves and subject them to the tests of reliability employed in general historiography and literary criticism. These tests are well set out by C. Sanders in his *Introduction to Research in English Literary History*[8] as "bibliographical," "internal" and "external." (Incidentally, since Sanders is a Professor of Military History, it seems unlikely that I can be criticized for theological bias in referring to him!)

## Bibliographical Test

The first test refers to the analysis of the textual tradition by which a document reaches us. In the case of the New Testament documents,

---

[8]C. Sanders, *Introduction to Research in English Literary History* (New York: The Macmillan Company, 1952), pp. 143 ff.

the question is: Can we arrive at a stable, reliable textual foundation for the claims of Jesus as set out in these records? The answer to this question is an unqualified "Yes." Sir Frederic G. Kenyon, formerly Director and Principal Librarian of the British Museum, summarizes the textual advantage which the New Testament documents have over all the other manuscripts of ancient classical authors:

> In no other case is the interval of time between the composition of the book and the date of the earliest extant manuscripts so short as in that of the New Testament. The books of the New Testament were written in the latter part of the first century; the earliest extant manuscripts (trifling scraps excepted) are of the fourth century—say, from 250 to 300 years later. This may sound a considerable interval, but it is nothing to that which parts most of the great classical authors from their earliest manuscripts. We believe that we have in all essentials an accurate text of the seven extant plays of Sophocles; yet the earliest substantial manuscript upon which it is based was written more than 1400 years after the poet's death. Aeschylus, Aristophanes, and Thucydides are in the same state; while with Euripides the interval is increased to 1600 years. For Plato it may be put at 1300 years, for Demosthenes as low as 1200.[9]

For confirmation of these intervals between date of composition and date of earliest substantial text, together with numerous other examples, see F.W. Hall's list.[10]

But even this is not the whole story. Since the time when Kenyon wrote the above words, numerous papyri portions of the New Testament documents have been discovered. These go back to the end of the first century, and bridge the 250 to 300 year gap of which Kenyon spoke. In evaluating these recent papyri discoveries, Kenyon concluded, shortly before his death:

---

[9]Frederic G. Kenyon, *Handbook to the Textual Criticism of the New Testament* (2nd. Ed.; London: The Macmillan Company, 1912), p. 5. See below, Appendix B, for Professor Edwin M. Yamauchi's evaluation of Kenyon's evidence.

[10]F.W. Hall, "MS Authorities for the Text of the Chief Classical Writers," in his *Companion to Classical Texts* (Oxford: Clarendon Press, 1913), pp. 199 ff.

The interval, then, between the dates of original composition and the earliest extant evidence becomes so small as to be in fact negligible, and the last foundation for any doubt that the Scriptures have come down to us substantially as they were written has now been removed. Both the authenticity and the general integrity of the books of the New Testament may be regarded as finally established.[11]

Moreover, as A.T. Robertson, the author of the most comprehensive grammar of New Testament Greek, wrote in his *Introduction to the Textual Criticism of the New Testament*:

There are some 8,000 manuscripts of the Latin Vulgate and at least 1,000 for the other early versions. Add over 4,000 Greek manuscripts and we have 13,000 manuscript copies of portions of the New Testament. Besides all this, much of the New Testament can be reproduced from the quotations of the early Christian writers.[12]

To express skepticism concerning the resultant text of the New Testament books (as represented, for example, by Nestle's *Novum Testamentum Graece*) is to allow all of classical antiquity to slip into obscurity, for no documents of the ancient period are as well attested bibliographically as the New Testament.

## Internal Evidence

The second test of documentary attribution and authenticity is that of internal evidence. Here historical and literary scholarship continues to follow Aristotle's eminently just dictum that the benefit of the doubt is to be given to the document itself, not arrogated by the critic to himself.[13] This means that one must listen to the claims of the document under analysis, and not assume fraud or error unless

---

[11]Frederic G. Kenyon, *The Bible and Archaeology* (New York and London: Harper and Row, 1940), pp. 288–289.

[12]A.T. Robertson, *Introduction to the Textual Criticism of the New Testament* (Nashville: Broadman Press, 1925), p. 70.

[13]See Aristotle, *Art of Poetry* (*De Arte Poetica*), 1460b–1461b.

the author disqualifies himself by contradictions or known factual inaccuracies. Thus, in the case of the Pauline letters, we must give considerable weight to their explicit claim to have been written by the Apostle. In the case of the whole gamut of New Testament documents, we must take the authors seriously when they say again and again that they are recording eyewitness testimony or testimony derived from equally reliable sources.

Examples can be multiplied. Here are but a few. Luke's Gospel begins with the words:

> Inasmuch as many have undertaken to compile a narrative of the things which have been accomplished among us, just as they were delivered to us by those who from the beginning were eyewitnesses and ministers of the word, it seemed good to me also, having followed all things closely for some time past, to write an orderly account for you, most excellent Theophilus, that you may know the truth concerning the things of which you have been informed.

The Fourth Gospel claims to have been written by an eyewitness to the crucifixion. In John 19:35 the author says, "He who saw it has borne witness—his testimony is true, and he knows that he tells the truth." 1 John, in its opening lines, likewise affirms eyewitness contact with Jesus:

> That which was from the beginning, which we have heard, which we have seen with our eyes, which we have looked upon and touched with our hands, concerning the word of life—the life was made manifest, and we saw it, and testify to it, and proclaim to you the eternal life which was with the Father and was made manifest to us—that which we have seen and heard we proclaim also to you.

Sometimes the internal evidence of primary historical authority is not as direct as in the above instances, but is no less decisive. For example, C.H. Turner[14] pointed out that Mark's Gospel reflects

---

[14]C.H. Turner, in Charles Gore *et al* eds., *A New Commentary on Holy Scripture* (London: SPCK, 1932), Pt III, pp. 42–124.

an eyewitness account of many scenes, for when the third person plural passes on to a third person singular involving Peter, we have the indirect equivalent of first person direct discourse, deriving from the Apostle. Such internal considerations, both direct and indirect, provide a weighty basis for the claim that the New Testament documents are reliable historical sources.

## External Evidence

Third, historians rely upon external evidence in matters of documentary authenticity or attribution. Here the question is asked: Do other historical materials confirm or deny the internal testimony provided by the documents themselves? Careful comparison of the New Testament documents with inscriptions and other independent early evidence has, in the modern period, confirmed their primary claims. For example, Sir William M. Ramsay came to his conclusion after years of painstaking archeological and geographical investigation of Luke's Gospel. He rejected the negatively critical attitude to Luke taken by the 19th century Tubingen school, and concluded, "Luke's history is unsurpassed in respect of its truthworthiness."[15]

Moreover, as to the authorship and primary historical value of the Gospel accounts, exceedingly valuable confirmation comes from independent written sources. Papias, bishop of Hierapolis around A.D. 130, writes as follows on the basis of information obtained from the "Elder" (Apostle) John. (I quote from Papias, as recorded in Eusebius' *Historia ecclesiastica*, III. 39):

> The Elder used to say this also: Mark, having been the interpreter of Peter, wrote down accurately all that he [Peter] mentioned, whether sayings or doings of Christ; not, however, in order. For he was neither a hearer nor a companion of the Lord; but afterwards, as I said, he accompanied Peter, who adapted his teachings as necessity required, not as though he were making a compilation of the sayings of the Lord. So then Mark made no mistake, writing down in this way some things as he [Peter] mentioned them; for he paid attention

---

[15]William M. Ramsay, *The Bearing of Recent Discovery on the Trustworthiness of the New Testament* (reprint ed.; Grand Rapids: Baker Book House, 1953), p. 81.

to this one thing, not to omit anything that he had heard, nor to include any false statement among them.

Of the Gospel according to Matthew, Papias says: "Matthew recorded the oracles in the Hebrew [i.e., Aramaic] tongue," and the acceptance the book received in the primitive Church argues strongly for its early date and historical value. McNeile and Williams write: "[Matthew's] Gospel was the first favourite in the early Church although it lacked the prestige of the two chief centers of Christendom, Rome and Ephesus; and the prestige also of the two chief apostolic names; Peter and Paul. And the strongly Judaic elements in it would have discredited it if it had appeared in the second century. All of which imply its early, widely known, and apostolic credit."[16]

Another superlative external testimony to the primacy of the Gospel accounts is provided by Irenaeus, bishop of Lyons, who writes:

> Matthew published his Gospel among the Hebrews [i.e., Jews] in their own tongue, when Peter and Paul were preaching the gospel in Rome and founding the church there. After their departure [i.e., death, which strong tradition places at the time of the Neronian persecution in 64], Mark, the disciple and interpreter of Peter, himself handed down to us in writing the substance of Peter's preaching. Luke, the follower of Paul, set down in a book the gospel preached by his teacher. Then John, the disciple of the Lord, who also leaned on his breast [this is a reference to John 13:25 and 21:20], himself produced his Gospel, while he was living at Ephesus in Asia.[17]

The value of Irenaeus' remarks is especially great because he had been a student of Polycarp, bishop of Smyrna (martyred in A.D. 156 after being a Christian for 86 years), and Polycarp in turn had been a disciple of the Apostle John himself. Irenaeus had often heard from Polycarp the eyewitness accounts of Jesus received from John and others who had been personally acquainted with Jesus.[18]

---

[16]McNeile and Williams, Introduction to the Study of the New Testament, p. 33.

[17]Irenaeus, *Adversus haereses*, III. 1 (ca. 180).

[18]See Eusebius, *Historia ecclesiastica*, V. 20.

On the basis, then, of powerful bibliographic, internal, and external evidence, competent historical scholarship must regard the New Testament documents as coming from the 1st century and as reflecting primary-source testimony about the person and claims of Jesus. Specifically, on the basis of such considerations as have just been set forth, present-day scholarship dates the more important New Testament materials as follows: the Pauline letters, 51–62; Mark's Gospel, 64–70; the Gospels according to Matthew and Luke, 80–85; Acts, shortly after Luke, which is really "Part One" of the two-part work; John's Gospel, no later than 100. It should be emphasized that the dates here given are in general the latest possible ones for the books in question. There is excellent reason for earlier dating in most cases (e.g., Luke-Acts should probably be dated prior to 64, since Paul almost certainly died in the Neronian persecution, yet Acts does not record his death). As a sensitive barometer to the current archeologically-based trend toward even earlier dating of these documents, we have the statement of the world's foremost biblical archeologist, W.F. Albright (whom, incidentally, Dr. Stroll cites at one point in his lecture, but not on this issue): "In my opinion, every book of the New Testament was written by a baptized Jew between the forties and the eighties of the first century A.D. (very probably sometime between about A.D. 50 and 75)."[19]

## Form Criticism

In the last chapter, I mentioned briefly Professor Stroll's heavy reliance upon the work of a radical school of New Testament critics, the so-called *formgeschichtliche Methode* school of Dibelius and Bultmann. We are now in a position to see why this school has been steadily losing ground in scholarly circles over the past few decades. The form critics attempt by literary analysis to "get behind" the New Testament documents as they have come down to us. The Gospels, for example, are assumed to be the end product of a process of oral tradition that was shaped and freely altered by the early Church according to its own needs—according to its *Sitz im Leben*.

---

[19]Quoted in an interview for *Christianity Today*, January 18, 1963.

Remarkably enough, this approach had already been flogged to death in the history of Homeric criticism, in an attempt to "get behind" the *Iliad* and the *Odyssey* as we have them. The result was complete chaos, for in the absence of any objective manuscript evidence to indicate where one "pre-literary" source left off and another began, the critics all differed with one another. H.J. Rose, in discussing the dreary history of the problem in his standard *Handbook of Greek Literature from Homer to the Age of Lucian*, writes:

> The chief weapon of the separatists has always been literary criticism, and of this it is not too much to say that such niggling word-baiting, such microscopic hunting of minute inconsistencies and flaws in logic, has hardly been seen, outside of the Homeric field, since Rymar and John Dennis died.[20]

In Dibelius, Bultmann and company, this kind of flaw hunting has been seen in the New Testament field since Rose's day, but its weaknesses are now widely recognized. The method depends on rationalistic presuppositions against the supernatural (as we previously indicated), and leaves the gates wide open to subjective interpretation. It principally falls down because the time interval between the writing of the New Testament documents as we have them and the events of Jesus' life which they record is too brief to allow for communal redaction by the Church.

John Drinkwater, in his *English Poetry*, has rejected this approach in the study of English ballads, and, as McNeile and Williams correctly note, "No Gospel section passed through such a long period of oral tradition as did any genuine ballad."[21]

This is not to say that New Testament writers did not ever employ sources. We have seen that Luke expressly asserts that he did so. But with the small time interval between Jesus' life and the Gospel records, the Church did not create a "Christ of faith" out of a simple, moralistic Jesus. We know from the Mishna that it was

---

[20]H.J. Rose, Handbook of Greek Literature from Homer to the Age of Lucian (London: Methuen, 1934), pp. 42–43.

[21]McNeile and Williams, Introduction to the Study of the New Testament, p. 58.

Jewish custom to memorize a Rabbi's teaching, for a good pupil was like a "plastered cistern that loses not a drop."[22] We can be sure that the early Church, impressed as it was by Jesus, governed itself by this ideal. Moreover—and of this Professor Stroll particularly should take note—none of the form-critical researches has ever been successful in yielding a non-supernatural picture of Jesus, for "all parts of the Gospel record are shown by these various groupings to be pervaded by a consistent picture of Jesus as the Messiah, the Son of God."[23]

## Conclusion

In conclusion, let us hear a clear statement of the implications of the evidence that has been presented. F.F. Bruce, whom we have just quoted, was one of the foremost contemporary experts on the Dead Sea Scrolls and served as Rylands Professor of Biblical Criticism and Exegesis in the University of Manchester. He writes as follows of the primary-source value of the New Testament records:

> The earliest preachers of the gospel knew the value of . . . firsthand testimony, and appealed to it time and again. "We are witnesses of these things," was their constant and confident assertion. And it can have been by no means so easy as some writers seem to think to invent words and deeds of Jesus in those early years, when so many of His disciples were about, who could remember what had and had not happened. Indeed, the evidence is that the early Christians were careful to distinguish between sayings of Jesus and their own inferences or judgments. Paul, for example, when discussing the vexed questions of marriage and divorce in 1 Corinthians 7, is careful to make the distinction between his own advice on the subject and the Lord's decisive ruling: "I, not the Lord," and again, "Not I, but the Lord."
> And it was not only friendly eyewitnesses that the early preachers had to reckon with; there were others less well-disposed who were also conversant with the main facts of the ministry and death of Jesus. The disciples could not afford to risk inaccuracies (not to speak of

---

[22]Mishna Aboth, II. 8.

[23]F.F. Bruce, *The New Testament Documents: Are They Reliable?* (5th ed.; London: Inter-Varsity Fellowship, 1960), p. 33.

willful manipulation of the facts), which would at once be exposed by those who would be only too glad to do so. On the contrary, one of the strong points in the original apostolic preaching is the confident appeal to the knowledge of the hearers; they not only said, "We are witnesses of these things," but also, "As you yourselves also know" (Acts 2: 22). Had there been any tendency to depart from the facts in any material respect, the possible presence of hostile witnesses in the audience would have served as a further corrective.[24]

What, then, does an historian know about Jesus Christ? He knows, first and foremost, that the New Testament documents can be relied upon to give an accurate portrait of him, and that this portrait cannot be rationalized away by wishful thinking, philosophical presuppositionalism or literary maneuvering. What exactly that portrait shows, and the radical consequences of it for each one of us will be set out in the next chapter.

---

[24]Bruce, The New Testament Documents, pp. 45–46.

# God Closes In

What can we know for sure about the historic Jesus? In the last chapter we discovered that on the basis of the accepted canons of historical method—bibliographic, internal and external evidence—the New Testament documents must be regarded as reliable sources of information. Indeed, we learned that the documentary attestation for these records is so strong that a denial of their reliability necessarily carries with it total skepticism toward the history and literature of the classical world. We found the New Testament books to contain eyewitness testimony to the life and claims of Jesus, and to have been in circulation while friends and foes who had known Jesus were still alive and able to refute exaggerated, inaccurate or unwarranted statements about him.

Now, if you are not inclined in the direction of Christianity—as I was not when I entered university—the most irritating aspect of the line of argument that I have taken is probably this: It depends in no sense on theology. It rests solely and squarely upon historical method, the kind of method all of us, whether Christians, rationalists, agnostics or Tibetan monks, have to use in analyzing historical data. Perhaps at this point we can understand why C.S. Lewis, the great Renaissance English scholar, in describing his conversion from atheism to Christianity, writes:

> Early in 1926 the hardest boiled of all the atheists I ever knew sat in my room on the other side of the fire and remarked that the evidence for the historicity of the Gospels was really surprisingly good. "Rum thing," he went on. "All that stuff of Frazer's about the Dying God. Rum thing. It almost looks as if it had really happened once." To understand the shattering impact of it, you would need to know the man (who has certainly never since shown any interest in Christianity). If he, the cynic of cynics, the toughest of the toughs, were

not—as I would still have put it—"safe", where could I turn? Was there then no escape?[25]

Subsequently, says Lewis, "God closed in on me." How "God closes in" when we face the implications of historically reliable New Testament documents is the subject of this chapter. We shall first examine the picture of Jesus in the primary documents that we have already validated. Then we shall consider the great evidential event, the Resurrection, which attests the claims Jesus made for himself and the religion which he proclaimed.

## The Divine Jesus of the Primary Documents

As we noted at the beginning of Chapter One, Jesus was especially concerned to bring his contemporaries to a sound and accurate conception of himself. We may assume that he would want us also to arrive at a conception of him that is consistent with his real personality. No one wants to be misunderstood; and surely it is vitally important in the case of a person such as Jesus, who has had such a tremendous influence on the history of the world, that misunderstanding be eliminated at all cost.

Yet in our day there has been a powerful tendency to create Jesus in the image of the time rather than to find out what the documents say about him. A bizarre, though in many ways typical, example is Bruce Barton's work, which attained great popularity in the mid-20th century, titled, *The Man Nobody Knows: A Discovery of the Real Jesus*. The title was more well chosen than Barton realized, for he clearly demonstrates that the Jesus of history is a man he doesn't know. Here are some representative chapter titles, referring to Jesus: "The Executive," "The Outdoor Man," "The Sociable Man," "The Founder of Modern Business." It is the last appellation that the author (himself, inevitably, a businessman) particularly stresses. Indeed, the book's title page quotation reads: "Wist ye not that I must be about my Father's business?"

---

[25]C.S. Lewis, *Surprised By Joy*, pp. 223–224.

But such dehistoricizings of Jesus are by no means limited to popular literature. Ironically, professional theologians have been more responsible than almost any other people in our day for producing unhistorical Jesuses. For example, we have the evaluation of Jesus given by Walter E. Bundy in his book, *The Religion of Jesus*:

> In our modern approach to Jesus we must leave him where and how and what he was, as real as he was—human . . . In all of his life and work Jesus placed himself on the side of humanity. Speculation only separates him from us and makes him increasingly unreal. There are very definite religious dangers in deification—dangers destructive of Christianity.[26]

As a liberal modern of the 20th century, Bundy paints a purely human portrait of Jesus, and warns against the dangers of regarding him as divine. But what, in fact, was Jesus like? Is he pictured in the reliable documentary sources as Barton's "business executive"? As Bundy's simple moral teacher, a Western Confucius going about giving people good advice that they didn't want anyway? Or as someone far different from the ideals of 20th century humanism?

To answer this question we must strike behind the welter of modern "reconstructions" of Jesus' life. We must go to the primary sources themselves. Only then will we avoid what C.S. Lewis in another work describes as the demonic creation of imaginary Jesuses. Screwtape, an elder devil, instructs his nephew on the fine art of anti-documentary temptation:

> In the last generation we promoted the construction of . . . a "historical Jesus" on liberal and humanitarian lines; we are now putting forward a new "historical Jesus" on Marxian, catastrophic, and revolutionary lines. The advantages of these constructions, which we intend to change every thirty years or so, are manifold. In the first place they all tend to direct men's devotion to something which does not exist, for each "historical Jesus" is unhistorical. The documents say what they say and cannot be added to; each new "historical Jesus" therefore has to be got out of them by suppression at one point and

---

[26]Walter E. Bundy, *The Religion of Jesus* (Indianapolis: Bobbs-Merrill, 1928), p. 324.

exaggeration at another, and by that sort of guessing (brilliant is the
adjective we teach humans to apply to it) on which no one would
risk ten shillings in ordinary life, but which is enough to produce a
crop of new Napoleons, new Shakespeares, and new Swifts in every
publisher's autumn list.[27]

In going to the documents to determine the *de facto* historical
picture of Jesus—as distinct from Screwtapean constructions—we
should keep two important caveats in mind. First, "red-letter" Bibles
notwithstanding, no attempt will be made to distinguish Jesus' conception of himself from the New Testament writers' conceptions of
him. All efforts to make such a distinction (and radical theological scholarship has frequently aimed at this kind of separation) are
pointless and doomed to failure from the outset, because Jesus' words
themselves have come to us by way of the New Testament writers.
The inability to distinguish Jesus' claims for himself from the New
Testament writers' claims for him, however, should cause no dismay,
since (1) the situation exactly parallels that for all historical personages who have not themselves chosen to write (e.g., Alexander the
Great, Augustus Caesar, Charlemagne). We would hardly claim that
in these cases we can achieve no adequate historical portraits. Also,
(2) the New Testament writers, as we saw in the previous chapter,
record eyewitness testimony concerning Jesus and can therefore be
trusted to convey an accurate historical picture of him.

A second preliminary caveat has to do with the approach we
take to discovering Jesus' nature. We have no right to begin with
the presupposition that Jesus can be no more than a man—for then,
obviously, our conclusions may simply reflect our preconceptions
instead of representing the actual content of the documents. We
must, in other words, objectively try to discover the Jesus of the primary historical records, whether we agree with them or not. The
question for us, it appears to me, is not whether Jesus is pictured as a
man. Virtually no one today would question this, for the records tell
us that he was hungry and tired; that he wept; that he suffered and
died—in short, that he was human. The question we face today is not

---

[27]C.S. Lewis, *The Screwtape Letters* (London: Bles, 1961), pp. 103–104.

whether he was a man, but whether he was depicted as no more than a man. It is instructive that the early church had to face the heresy of docetism, which did question Jesus' humanity. The docetists were so impressed by the evidence for Jesus' divinity that to them he only "seemed" (Greek: *dokein*) to be a man. But for us as humanistically-oriented moderns, the divinity of Jesus is the question, and only the documents can provide the answer to it.

What do the documents say? They say unequivocally and consistently that Jesus regarded himself as no less than God in the flesh, and that his disciples, under the pressure of his own words and deeds, came to regard him in this same way. Let us consider the prime New Testament records, in chronological order, and follow them by a significant passage from an early non-biblical source.

### The Letters of Paul

We begin with the letters of Paul, since, as we pointed out in the last chapter, they are the earliest materials we possess that bear on primitive Christianity. They date from between A.D. 51 and 62, and are firmly wedded to the Gospel records by way of Luke-Acts, where the stamp of approval is placed upon Paul by the original apostles. We can thus quote Paul without hesitation. Baur and the Tubingen school of the 19th century were unsuccessful in driving a wedge between Jesus and Paul, and present-day biblical scholarship has rejected their approach and conclusions (see J.G. Machen's classic, *The Origin of Paul's Religion*).[28]

In Paul's writings the divine character of Jesus is affirmed in three unequivocal ways. (1) Paul applies to Jesus the Greek word *kyrios* ("Lord"), which was used in the pre-Christian Greek translation of the Old Testament (the Septuagint) as the equivalent of the Hebrew name of God, *Jehovah* (better, *Yahweh* or YHWH).[29] Note the implications of this: Paul, a monotheistic Jew, trained under the great Rabbi Gamaliel

---

[28]J.G. Machen, *The Origin of Paul's Religion* (Grand Rapids: Eerdmans, 1965).

[29]The Hebrew word *YHWH* was actually not pronounced in Old Testament times, out of reverence. Instead, the vowels for the Hebrew word "Lord"—*Adonai*—were given it, and *Adonai* was substituted in public reading. Thus it was natural for the Hellenistic Jews who prepared the Septuagint—in Alexandria, from ca. 300 to

and therefore thoroughly conversant with the Old Testament, ascribes to Jesus a word employed to render into Greek the most holy name of the one God!

Consider as an example of Paul's identification of Jesus with the God of the Old Testament the following passages:

> Turn to me and be saved, all the ends of the earth! For I am God, and there is no other. By myself I have sworn, from my mouth has gone forth in righteousness a word that shall not return: "To me every knee shall bow, every tongue shall swear." (Isaiah 45:22–23)

> At the name of Jesus every knee should bow, in heaven and on earth and under the earth, and every tongue confess that Jesus Christ is Lord [*kyrios*], to the glory of God the Father. (Philippians 2:10–11)

Here Paul takes an Old Testament passage expressing in the most lofty and explicit terms the majesty and oneness of God, and applies it directly to Jesus, whom he refers to as *kyrios*. Instances of this kind can be multiplied with ease; see, for example, 2 Thessalonians 1:9 (quoting Isaiah 2:10, 19, 21); 1 Corinthians 1:31 and 2 Corinthians 10:17 (quoting Jeremiah 9:23 ff.); 1 Corinthians 10:9 (quoting Numbers 21:5 ff.).[30]

(2) With the phrases "Our God and Father and our Lord Jesus Christ" (1 Thessalonians 3:11) and "Our Lord Jesus Christ and God our Father" (2 Thessalonians 2:16), Paul uses a singular verb. This makes patently clear that for him, Jesus and the God of the Old Testament were conceived of as an essential unity. This conclusion is made even stronger (if it were possible!) by the fact that both phrases appear in prayers. Thus Paul believed that prayer could be directed indiscriminately to God the Father or Jesus.

(3) Paul held that Jesus would reappear as divine Judge at the end of the age:

---

ca. 100 B.C.—to use *kyrios* in rendering into Greek the Hebrew *YHWH*. (For another view of this linguistic point, see C.S. Lewis' letter on page 8.)

[30]See also the composite work, *Who Say Ye That I Am?*, ed. W.C. Robinson (Grand Rapids: Eerdmans, 1949), pp. 133 ff.

. . . when the Lord Jesus is revealed from heaven with his mighty angels in flaming fire, inflicting vengeance upon those who do not know God and upon those who do not obey the gospel of our Lord Jesus. They shall suffer the punishment of eternal destruction and exclusion from the presence of the Lord and from the glory of his might, when he comes on that day to be glorified in his saints, and to be marveled at in all who have believed, because our testimony to you was believed. (2 Thessalonians 1:7–10)

## Mark

Next let us look at the earliest of the four Gospels, Mark, which was written no later than A.D. 64–70 by a companion of the apostle Peter. At the very outset of this book Mark makes clear beyond all shadow of doubt that Jesus should be personally identified with the God of the Old Testament. He writes:

The beginning of the gospel of Jesus Christ, the Son of God. As it is written in Isaiah the prophet, "Behold, I send my messenger before thy face, who shall prepare thy way; the voice of one crying in the wilderness: Prepare the way of the Lord, make his paths straight." (Mark 1:1–3)

Here Mark has quoted Malachi 3:1, but with a highly significant alteration. The prophetic verse reads: "Behold, I [Jehovah] send my messenger to prepare the way before me." But Mark changes the verse so that it reads "he shall prepare thy way," that is, Jesus' way. Mark is saying, in other words, that when the God of the prophets spoke of preparing for his own coming, he was speaking of the preparation for Jesus' coming; or, putting it as simply as possible, Jesus is the God of the prophets.

This affirmation, which in the Greek text of Mark stands like a red flare at the beginning of the book, is confirmed again and again throughout the book. In chapter 2, Jesus forgives sin—and the scribes recognize, correctly, that he is blaspheming if he is not God, for only God can forgive sins.

And when he returned to Capernaum after some days, it was reported that he was at home. And many were gathered together, so that there was no longer room for them, not even about the door;

and he was preaching the word to them. And they came, bringing to him a paralytic carried by four men. And when they could not get near him because of the crowd, they removed the roof above him; and when they had made an opening, they let down the pallet on which the paralytic lay. And when Jesus saw their faith, he said to the paralytic, "My son, your sins are forgiven." Now some of the Scribes were sitting there, questioning in their hearts, "Why does this man speak thus? It is blasphemy! Who can forgive sins but God alone?" And immediately Jesus, perceiving in his spirit that they thus questioned within themselves, said to them, "Why do you question thus in your hearts? Which is easier, to say to the paralytic, 'Your sins are forgiven,' or to say, 'Rise, take up your pallet and walk'? But that you may know that the Son of man has authority on earth to forgive sins"—he said to the paralytic—"I say to you, rise, take up your pallet and go home." And he rose, and immediately took up the pallet and went out before them all; so that they were all amazed and glorified God, saying, "We never saw anything like this!" (Mark 2:1–12)

But is Jesus not perhaps regarding himself simply as a man with special privileges? Does he not use the expression "Son of man"? This expression, which humanists have often appealed to as equivalent to "representative humanity," is really one of the loftiest ascriptions given to God's Messiah in the Old Testament (see Daniel 7:13). Jesus expressly applies this imagery to himself at his trial, and brings upon himself condemnation for—let it be noted—blasphemy.

Again the high priest asked him, "Are you the Christ, the Son of the Blessed?" And Jesus said, "I am; and you will see the Son of man sitting at the right hand of Power, and coming with the clouds of heaven." And the high priest tore his mantle, and said, "Why do we still need witnesses? You have heard his blasphemy. What is your decision?" And they all condemned him as deserving death. (Mark 14:61–64)

Although not much good can be said about the high priest at this kangaroo court, one thing is certain: He correctly recognized that Jesus was claiming to be no less than God incarnate, and if he was not what he claimed, then he was a blasphemer.

## Matthew

The Gospels according to Matthew (the apostle) and Luke (a physician who accompanied Paul on his missionary journeys) were written no later than A.D. 80–85. Albright would say probably before 75. They present the same divine-human picture of Jesus given in Mark. The virgin birth account in these two Gospels is unequivocal. Even though the Hebrew word *almah* in the Isaiah prophecy can mean "young woman" as well as "virgin," the Greek *parthenos* employed in Matthew and Luke must mean "virgin." As Karl Barth has correctly noted, the virgin birth demonstrates that God the Father uniquely entered history in Jesus and was the active agent in his advent. Moreover, the Jesus of these Gospels makes absolute claims for himself that are unthinkable apart from deity. For example, Jesus says:

> So every one who acknowledges me before men, I also will acknowledge before my Father who is in heaven; but whoever denies me before men, I also will deny before my Father who is in heaven . . . He who finds his life will lose it, and he who loses his life for my sake will find it. (Matthew 10:32–33, 39)

Jesus states his divine life-purpose as follows: "The Son of man came . . . to give his life as a ransom for many" (Matthew 20:28), and this assertion is also integral to Mark's Gospel (Mark 10:45). Jesus' last words in the Gospel according to Matthew are also consonant only with deity, for they ascribe to him the divine attributes of omnipotence and omnipresence and place him on the same plane as the Father:

> And Jesus came and said to them, "All authority in heaven and on earth has been given to me. Go therefore, and make disciples of all nations, baptizing them in the name of the Father and of the Son and of the Holy Spirit, teaching them to observe all that I have commanded you; and lo, I am with you always, to the close of the age." (Matthew 28:18–20)

## Acts

In the Book of Acts, written by Luke, Paul is converted to Christianity in the recognition, on the Damascus road, that Jesus is *kyrios*

(Acts 9:5). The entire apostolic preaching, as C.H. Dodd has so effectively pointed out, centers on the Lordship of Jesus.[31] "What must I do to be saved?" is the question. "Believe in the Lord Jesus and you will be saved" is the consistent answer (cf. Acts 16:30–31). Indeed, "there is salvation in no one else, for there is no other name under heaven given among men by which we must be saved" (Acts 4:12).

*John*

The fourth Gospel is thoroughly Christocentric, and identifies the Eternal Father with the historic Jesus at every point. The Prologue affirms Jesus' pre-existence and eternal oneness with God. The "I am" sayings ("I am the light, bread," etc.) allude to the "I am that I am" revelations of the God of the Old Testament (see Exodus 3:14).[32] Salvation occurs only through Jesus. He says in John 14:6, "I am the way, and the truth, and the life; no one comes to the Father, but by me." And the numerous miracle-signs performed by Jesus in this Gospel, culminating in the great sign—the resurrection—are recorded "that you may believe that Jesus is the Christ, the Son of God, and that believing you may have life in his name." (John 20:31). Indeed, the Gospel reaches its climax with the "doubting Thomas" incident, in which Thomas is confronted by the resurrected Jesus and confesses, "My Lord and my God." (John 20:28) This picture of Jesus in John's Gospel is especially meaningful when we remember that the apostolic authorship of the book is attested by Irenaeus, who knew Polycarp, a disciple of John himself.

## Conclusion

Thus a consistent portrait of Jesus emerges from the earliest New Testament documents: a divine portrait of one who could say, "He who has seen me has seen the Father" (John 14:9). And this is how

---

[31]C.H. Dodd, *The Apostolic Preaching and Its Developments*, (New York: Harper & Row, 1964).

[32]Incidentally, there is almost certainly an etymological connection between the Hebrew name of God, *YHWH*, and the Hebrew verb "am"—*HYH*; cf. with Exodus 3:14 the parallel verse, Exodus 6:3.

Christians from the earliest days have regarded him. In the first description of Christian worship from the pen of a non-Christian we read: "On an appointed day they [Christians] were accustomed to meet before daybreak, and to recite a hymn antiphonally to Christ, as to God." This significant passage comes from a letter written ca. 112 by the governor of Bithynia, Pliny the Younger, to the Emperor Trajan (*Epis.* X, xcvi). From that day to this all Christians—Eastern Orthodox, Roman Catholic and Protestant—have worshipped Christ as God on the basis of the historically impeccable testimony of Jesus' own followers and of those who knew them intimately.

The Jesus of the primary documents, then, is one hundred and eighty degrees removed from the "businessman" of Barton, the humanistic moralist of Bundy, the catastrophic reformer of the Marxists, and from all other modern attempts to create him in the image of cultural idealism. We may not like the Jesus of the historical documents; but like him or not, we meet him there as a divine being on whom our personal destiny, both in time and in eternity, depends.

# An Historian's Appeal

Granted that the New Testament documents portray a divine Christ; was he in fact divine? Logically, if Jesus was not divine, as the records unequivocally claim he was, we are reduced to three, and only three, interpretations of the New Testament data:

1. Jesus claimed to be the Son of God, but knew he was not. He was a charlatan.
2. Jesus thought he was the Son of God, but actually he was not. He was a lunatic.
3. Jesus never actually claimed to be the Son of God, though his disciples put this claim in his mouth. So, the disciples were charlatans, lunatics, or naive exaggerators.

I believe that a careful consideration of these three interpretations will show that no one of them is consonant with history, psychology or reason, and that therefore, by process of elimination, we are brought to affirm Jesus' deity not only as a claim, but also as a fact.

## Charlatan?

The idea of Jesus as a charlatan—as an intentional deceiver who claimed to be something he knew he was not—has never had much appeal, even among fanatical anti-religionists. Jesus' high ethical teachings and noble personal character have made such an interpretation improbable in the extreme. W.E.H. Lecky, the great 19th century historian and certainly no believer in revealed religion, wrote thus of Jesus in his *History of European Morals from Augustus to Charlemagne*:

The character of Jesus has not only been the highest pattern of virtue, but the strongest incentive to its practice, and has exerted so deep an influence, that it may be truly said, that the simple record of three short years of active life has done more to regenerate and to soften mankind, than all the disquisitions of philosophers and than all the exhortations of moralists.[33]

This judgment has been echoed thousands of times through the centuries by men of all or no religious persuasions. Is it possible that such a Jesus would have committed one of the most basic moral errors of all—allowing the end to justify the means—and based his entire life and ethical teachings upon a colossal lie as to his real nature? He was at pains to convince the men of his time that the devil is a liar and the father of lies, and that those who lie are the devil's children (John 8:44). Would he himself then have lied concerning the essence of his own character and purpose? To answer anything but an unqualified "No" is to renounce sound ethical judgment.

## Lunatic?

But perhaps Jesus' claims to deity and messiahship had their source not in intentional deception, but in Jesus' honest misunderstanding of his nature. This is the position taken by Schweitzer in 1906 in his *Geschichte der Leben-Jesu-Forschung* (translated into English by William Montgomery and published in 1910 as *The Quest of the Historical Jesus*), a work which was epochal because of its recognition of the eschatological character of Jesus' message, but which is almost universally regarded by New Testament scholars today as setting out an "historical Jesus" who reflects Schweitzer's own rationalistic presuppositions.

Now it is of real interest that Schweitzer felt it necessary to vindicate his Jesus (who misunderstood his own nature) from the charge of psychiatric illness. Schweitzer's *Psychiatric Study of Jesus* (his Strasbourg M.D. dissertation of 1913) is an herculean, but ineffective

---

[33]W.E.H. Lecky, *History of European Morals from Augustus to Charlemagne* (2nd. Ed.; London: Longmans, Green, 1869), II, p. 88.

attempt to show that the purely human Jesus could be sane and yet think of himself as the eschatological Son of man who would come again at the end of the age, with the heavenly host, to judge the world. In actuality, as Dr. Winfred Overholser, past president of the American Psychiatric Association, has noted in his foreword to the latest English edition of Schweitzer's thesis, Schweitzer has not ruled out paranoia in the case of a purely human Jesus: "Some paranoids manifest ideas of grandeur almost entirely, and we find patients whose grandeur is very largely of a religious nature, such as their belief that they are directly instructed by God to convert the world or perform miracles."[34]

We cannot avoid the conclusion that Jesus was deranged if he thought of himself as God incarnate and yet was not. Noyes and Kolb, in the 5th edition of their standard medical text, *Modern Clinical Psychiatry*, characterize the schizophrenic as one whose behavior becomes autistic rather than realistic, one who allows himself to "retreat from the world of reality."[35] What greater retreat from reality is there than a belief in one's divinity, if one is not in fact God? I know that you would immediately summon the men in white coats if I—or anyone else—seriously made the claims for myself that Jesus did! Yet, in view of the eminent soundness of Jesus' teachings, few have been able to give credence to the idea of mental aberration. Indeed, the psychiatrist J.T. Fisher has asserted what many others have been implicitly convinced of:

If you were to take the sum total of all authoritative articles ever written by the most qualified of psychologists and psychiatrists on the subject of mental hygiene—if you were to combine them and refine them and cleave out the excess verbiage—if you were to take the whole of the meat and none of the parsley, and if you were to have these unadulterated bits of pure scientific knowledge concisely expressed by the most capable of living poets, you would have an awkward and incomplete summation of the Sermon on the Mount. And it would suffer immeasurably through comparison. For nearly

[34]Albert Schweitzer, *The Psychiatric Study of Jesus* (Boston: Beacon Press, 1958), p. 15.

[35]Noyes and Kolb, *Modern Clinical Psychiatry* (Philadelphia and London: Saunders, 1958), p. 401.

two thousand years the Christian world has been holding in its hands
the complete answer to its restless and fruitless yearnings. Here . . .
rests the blueprint for successful human life with optimum mental
health and contentment.[36]

But one cannot very well have it both ways. If Jesus' teachings
provide "the blueprint for successful human life with optimum mental health," then the teacher cannot be a lunatic who totally mis-
understands the nature of his own personality. Note the absolute
dichotomy: If the documentary records of Jesus' life are accurate,
and Jesus was not a charlatan, then he was either God incarnate as
he claimed or a psychotic. If we cannot take the latter alternative
(and, considering its consequences, who really can follow this path
to its logical conclusion?), we must arrive at a Jesus who claimed to
be God incarnate simply because he was God.

## False Portrait?

But, is there not a third way of escaping the horns of this dilemma?
Could not Jesus' followers have painted a false portrait of him—out
of an intentional or unintentional desire to put him in the best possible light? This, you will remember, is Professor Stroll's main con-
tention: that a "messianic fever" pervaded the Jews under 1st century
Roman domination, and led some of them to deify Jesus of Nazareth.
This interpretation, though perhaps superficially plausible, has no
more to commend it than the interpretations we have just considered. It falls down on three decisive counts. (1) All types of Jewish
messianic speculation at the time were at variance with the messianic picture Jesus painted of himself, so he was a singularly poor
candidate for deification. (2) The apostles and evangelists were psychologically, ethically and religiously incapable of performing such a
deification. (3) The historical evidence for Christ's resurrection—the
great attesting event for his claims to deity—could not have been
manufactured. Let us take up each of these in turn.

---

[36]J.T. Fisher and L.S. Hawley, *A Few Buttons Missing* (Philadelphia: J.B. Lippincott,
1951), p. 273.

In order for the Jews of Jesus' time to have messianized him, it would have been necessary for Jesus' teachings and conception of himself to accord with the main outlines of the messianic hope held by his contemporaries. However, in all essential points this was not the case. Consider, for example, Jesus' attitude toward the Gentiles. Edersheim, late Grinfield Lecturer on the Septuagint at Oxford, writes in his *Sketches of Jewish Social Life in the Days of Christ*:

> In view of all this [first century Jewish antipathy toward the heathen in Palestine], what an almost incredible truth must it have seemed, when the Lord Jesus Christ proclaimed it among Israel as the object of His coming and kingdom, not to make of the Gentiles Jews, but of both alike children of one Heavenly Father; not to rivet upon the heathen the yoke of the law, but to deliver from it Jew and Gentile, or rather to fulfil its demands for all! The most unexpected and unprepared-for revelation, from the Jewish point of view, was that of the breaking down of the middle wall of partition between Jew and Gentile, the taking away of the enmity of the law, and the nailing it to his cross. There was nothing analogous to it; not a hint of it to be found, either in the teaching or the spirit of the times. Quite the opposite. Assuredly, the most unlike thing to Christ were his times.[37]

The great Jewish scholar S.W. Baron, in his widely acclaimed *Social and Religious History of the Jews*,[38] presents a detailed discussion of "Messianic Expectations" at the time of Jesus. He writes that "Zealot activists expected the redeemer to appear sword in hand and to lead the people against Rome's military power"; that "most apocalyptic visionaries, on the other hand, expected redemption in the shape of a cosmic cataclysm, out of which would emerge a new world with the chosen people marching toward final salvation at the head of a transformed mankind"; and that even those with "less high-flown expectations" were convinced that the messiah would bring back "the remnants of the lost Ten Tribes" and reunite Israel and

---

[37]Edersheim, *Sketches of Jewish Social Life in the Days of Christ* (reprint ed.; Grand Rapids: Eerdmans, 1957), pp. 28–29.

[38]S.W. Baron, *Social and Religious History of the Jews* (2nd ed.; New York: Columbia University Press, 1952), II, pp. 58 ff.

Judah. Does this sound like the Jesus of the documents who said, "My kingdom is not of this world"? Baron regards Jesus "as an essentially Pharisaic Jew,"[39] but the primary records present the Pharisees as his chief opponents. He continually set himself above the law and refused to be bound by the legalistic traditions of the Pharisees.

As for the party of the Sadducees, no one would argue that common ground existed between Jesus and them, for they were rationalistically inclined. (They denied the general resurrection of the body, the existence of angels, etc.) And though mutual hate and mistrust colored the relations between Pharisees and Sadducees, both parties were so disturbed by Jesus that they united against him (Matthew 16:1, etc.). The single fact that official Jewry crucified Jesus for blasphemy is sufficient ground for rejecting the idea that Jesus fulfilled the messianic dreams of the time!

But what about the Essene sect of the Dead Sea Scrolls, to which Professor Stroll makes reference? Millar Burrows[40] and F.F. Bruce,[41] among other experts on the Scrolls, have shown beyond question that the Essene conception of a "Teacher of Righteousness" differed in all essential points from Jesus' messianic views. Burrows demonstrates among other things that "there is no hint of a pre-existent Messiah in the Qumran texts"; that "nowhere is there a suggestion of anything miraculous in the birth of the teacher of righteousness"; that "the saving efficacy of the death of Christ has no parallel in the beliefs of the covenanters concerning either the teacher of righteousness or the coming Messiah" (indeed, that "the idea of a suffering Messiah . . . was known at all in Judaism at that time is a debatable question"). Moreover, since the teacher of righteousness was not believed to rise from the dead until the general resurrection at the end of the age, whereas Jesus was believed to have risen directly following his crucifixion, "what for the community of Qumran was at most a hope was for the Christians an accomplished fact, the guarantee of all their hopes."

---

[39] Baron, *Social and Religious History of the Jews*, p. 67.

[40] Millar Burrows, *More Light on the Dead Sea Scrolls* (New York: Viking Press, 1958), pp. 65–73.

[41] F.F. Bruce, *Second Thoughts on the Dead Sea Scrolls* (London: Paternoster Press, 1956), *passim*.

Burrows goes on to show that "the term which Jesus most commonly used in referring to himself ('Son of man') is one that does not occur at all in the Qumran literature as a Messianic designation," and—what is perhaps most significant of all—"there is no indication that the teacher of righteousness was considered divine in any sense." To argue, then, that Jesus was deified or messianized because he fulfilled Essene messianic expectation is impossible on historical ground.

Note the point at which we have arrived: if anyone deified Jesus, it must have been his own disciples—against the entire pressure of first century Jewish ideology. But, as Burrows correctly states: "Jesus was so unlike what all Jews expected the son of David to be that his own disciples found it almost impossible to connect the idea of the Messiah with him."[42] And even when they did become convinced that he was God's anointed, could they have deified him without cause? R.T. Herford, in discussing "The Influence of Judaism upon Jews from Hillel to Mendelssohn," says: "The Jewish religion throughout the whole of the period is based upon two main principles, the assertion of the undivided unity of God and the paramount duty of obedience to His declared Will."[43] Would then the disciples and followers of Jesus—steeped in the Jewish faith—have deified a mere man, thereby contradicting the central tenet of the Jewish faith, that "you shall have no other gods before me"?

Furthermore, were these early followers of Jesus psychologically or temperamentally capable of carrying out such a deification process? Certainly they—no more than Jesus himself—were charlatans or psychotics. The picture of them in the documents is one of practical, ordinary people—down-to-earth fishermen, hardheaded tax gatherers, etc.—and people with perhaps more than the usual dose of skepticism. (Think of Peter returning to his old way of life after Jesus' death, and "doubting" Thomas.) Hardly the kind of men to be swept off their feet into mass hallucination of technicolor proportions!

What did finally and irrevocably convince the followers of Jesus that he was the one he claimed to be, God incarnate? What

---

[42]Burrows, *More Light on the Dead Sea Scrolls*, p. 68.

[43]R.T. Herford, *Legacy of Israel* (Oxford: Clarendon Press, 1928), p. 103.

transformed them from a shocked and broken group after the crucifixion to a company that preached Jesus' message of salvation up and
down the Roman world until the empire itself, and with it the Western world, became Christian? The answer lies in the resurrection,
and a brief discussion of it will conclude our presentation.

## The Resurrection

Jesus was crucified in Jerusalem during the high festival of the Jewish
religious year—the Passover. The city was teeming with people, and
because of the involvement of mobs in the quasi-legal proceedings,
it is clear that the public was well aware of what was transpiring.
Owing to the fact that Jesus had claimed that he would rise again
after three days, and indeed had pointed to this event as the final
proof of his claims to deity (Matthew 12:38–40; John 2:18–22), the
Jewish religious leaders made certain that guards were stationed
at the tomb to prevent the disciples from stealing Jesus' body and
maintaining that he had actually risen. However, according to the
documents, Jesus did rise—bodily—and was seen again and again
over a forty-day period, until he publicly ascended into heaven. The
appearances are recorded with clinical detail:

> As they [the disciples] were saying this, Jesus himself stood among
> them. But they were startled and frightened, and supposed that they
> saw a spirit. And he said to them, "Why are you troubled, and why
> do questionings rise in your hearts? See my hands and my feet, that
> it is I myself; handle me, and see; for a spirit has not flesh and bones
> as you see that I have." And while they still disbelieved for joy, and
> wondered, he said to them, "Have you anything here to eat?" They
> gave him a piece of broiled fish, and he took it and ate before them.
> (Luke 24:36–43)

> So the other disciples told him [Thomas], "We have seen the Lord."
> But he said to them, "Unless I see in his hands the print of the nails,
> and place my finger in the mark of the nails, and place my hand in
> his side, I will not believe." Eight days later, his disciples were again in
> the house, and Thomas was with them. The doors were shut, but Jesus
> came and stood among them, and said, "Peace be with you." Then he

said to Thomas, "Put your finger here, and see my hands; and put out your hand, and place it in my side; do not be faithless, but believing." Thomas answered him, "My Lord and my God!" (John 20:25–28)

The records leave no doubt that the writers were well aware of the distinction between myth and fact, and that they were proclaiming the resurrection as factual. "We," they write, "did not follow cleverly devised myths when we made known to you the power and coming of our Lord Jesus Christ, but we were eyewitnesses of his majesty" (2 Peter 1:16). The facticity of the resurrection provided the disciples with the final proof of the truth of Jesus' claim to deity. It provides the historian with the only adequate explanation for the conquering power of Christianity after the death of its founder. False messiahs of the time fell into obscurity because they could not back up their claims. For example, Theudas in A.D. 44 promised a crowd that he would divide the waters of the Jordan River, and in A.D. 52–54 an unnamed "Egyptian" messiah gathered a crowd of 30,000 Jews and said that at his command the walls of Jerusalem would fall down—but both incidents ended in ignominious failure, accompanied by bloodshed at the hands of the Roman soldiery.[44] Christianity, however, flourished as a result of Jesus' attested claim to conquer the power of death.

But can the modern man accept a "miracle" such as the resurrection? The answer is a surprising one. The resurrection has to be accepted by us just because we are modern men—men living in the Einsteinian-relativistic age. For us, unlike people of the Newtonian epoch, the universe is no longer a tight, safe, predictable playing field in which we know all the rules. Since Einstein, no modern has had the right to rule out the possibility of events because of prior knowledge of "natural law." The only way we can know whether an event can occur is to see whether in fact it has occurred. The problem of "miracles," then, must be solved in the realm of historical investigation, not in the realm of philosophical speculation. And note that an historian, in facing an alleged "miracle," is really facing nothing new. All historical events are unique, and the test of their facticity can be

---

[44]Josephus, *Jewish War*, II, 13, 4. 259; *Antiquities*, XX, 8, 6. 170.

only the accepted documentary approach that we have followed here. No historian has a right to a closed system of natural causation, for as the Cornell logician Max Black has shown, the very concept of cause is "a peculiar, unsystematic, and erratic notion," and therefore "any attempt to state a 'universal law of causation' must prove futile."[45]

As Ethelbert Stauffer, the Erlangen historian, puts it: "What do we do [as historians] when we experience surprises which run counter to all our expectations, perhaps all our convictions and even our period's whole understanding of truth? We say as one great historian used to say in such instances: 'It is surely possible.' And why not? For the critical historian nothing is impossible."[46] If the resurrection did occur—and the evidence for it is tremendous—then we cannot rule it out because we are unable to "explain" it by an *a priori* causal schema. Rather, we must go to the one who rose to find the explanation—and his explanation, though we may not like it, is that only God himself, the Lord of life, could conquer the powers of death.

Of course, attempts have been made to "explain" the resurrection accounts naturalistically. The German rationalist Venturini suggested in all seriousness that Jesus only fainted on the cross and subsequently revived in the cool tomb. This "swoon theory" is typical of all such arguments: They are infinitely more improbable than the resurrection itself, and they fly squarely in the face of the documentary evidence. Jesus surely died on the cross, for Roman crucifixion teams knew their business—they had enough practice! He could not possibly have rolled the heavy boulder from the door of the tomb after the crucifixion experience. And even if we discounted these immense improbabilities, what happened to him later?

If we agree that he died and was interred, then the occasionally alleged "explanation" that the body was stolen is no more helpful. For who would have taken it? Surely not the Romans or the Jewish parties, for they wished at all costs to squelch the Christian sect. And certainly not the Christians, for to do so and then fabricate detailed accounts of Jesus' resurrection would have been to fly in the face of

[45]Max Black, *Models and Metaphors* (Ithaca: Cornell University Press, 1962), p. 169.
[46]Ethelbert Stauffer, *Jesus and His Story* (New York: Knopf, 1960), p. 17.

the ethic their master preached and for which they ultimately died. As J.V. Langmead Casserley pointed out in his 1951 Maurice Lectures at King's College, London, the attempts to explain away the resurrection demonstrate that "the assertion of the resurrection is like a knife pointed at the throat of the irreligious man, and an irreligious man whose irreligion is threatened will fight for his own creation, his most precious possession, like a tigress fighting for her cubs."[47]

Note well that when the disciples of Jesus proclaimed the resurrection, they did so as eyewitnesses and they did so while people were still alive who had had contact with the events of which they spoke. In A.D. 56, Paul wrote that over 500 people had seen the risen Jesus and that most of them were still alive (1 Corinthians 15:1 ff). It passes the bounds of credibility that the early Christians could have manufactured such a tale and then preached it among those who might easily have refuted it simply by producing the body of Jesus.[48]

The conclusion? Jesus did rise, and thereby validated his claim to divinity. He was neither charlatan nor lunatic, and his followers were not fable-mongers; they were witnesses to the incarnation of God, and Jesus was the God of whom they testified.

## An Historian's Appeal

Today, especially in university circles, agnosticism has become immensely fashionable. The days of the hidebound atheist appear to be past, but his agnostic replacement is in many ways even farther from the intellectual mainline. The atheist at least has recognized the necessity of taking a position on ultimate matters. The agnostic, however, frequently makes a demi-god out of indecision. Actually—as Heidegger, Sartre and other contemporary existentialists stress—all life is decision, and no man can sit on the fence. To do so is really to make a decision—a decision against decision. Historians, and indeed all of us, must make decisions constantly, and the only

---

[47]J.V. Langmead Casserly, *The Retreat from Christianity in the Modern World* (London: Longmans, Green, 1952), p. 82.

[48]Frank Morison, *Who Moved the Stone?* (new ed.; London: Faber and Faber, 1944), *passim*.

adequate guide is probability—since absolute certainty lies only in the realms of pure logic and mathematics, where, by definition, one encounters no matters of fact at all. I have tried to show that the weight of historical probability lies on the side of the validity of Jesus' claim to be God incarnate, the Savior of man, and the coming Judge of the world. If probability does in fact support these claims—and can we really deny it, having studied the evidence?—then we must act in behalf of them. When Jesus said that he would spew the luke-warm out of his mouth (Revelation 3:16), he was saying that action on his claims is mandatory. "He who is not with me is against me," he plainly taught.

And how do we act in behalf of his claims? In just one way. We come to the point of acknowledging that the ultimate problems of our existence, such as death and the self-centeredness that gives death its sting, can only be solved in his presence. We look away from ourselves to his death and resurrection for the answers to our deepest needs. We put ourselves into his hands.

What is the result of such a personal commitment to the risen Christ? I can myself attest to it. Freedom—for the servant of Christ is slave to no man. In a fearfully changing world, he is solidly grounded in an unchanging Christ, and therefore is free to develop his capacities to the fullest, under God. If, again to use C.S. Lewis' words, God has "closed in on you," why not let the gap be closed entirely? As Pascal so well put it, you have nothing to lose and everything to gain.

# Legal Evidence

# Christianity Juridically Defended

Existential, blind "leaps of faith" can be and often are suicide jumps, with no criteria of truth available before the leap is made. But suppose the truth of a religious claim did not depend upon an unverifiable, subjectivistic leap of faith? What if a revelational truth-claim did not turn on questions of theology and religious philosophy—on any kind of esoteric, fideistic method available only to those who are already "true believers"—but on the very reasoning employed in the law to determine questions of fact?

The historic Christian claim differs qualitatively from the claims of all other world religions at the epistemological point: on the issue of testability. Eastern faiths and Islam, to take familiar examples, ask the uncommitted seeker to discover their truth experientially: the faith-experience will be self-validating. Unhappily, as analytical philosopher Kai Nielsen and others have rigorously shown, a subjective faith-experience is logically incapable of "validating God-talk"—including the alleged absolutes about which the god in question does the talking.[49] Christianity, on the other hand, declares that the truth of its absolute claims rests squarely on certain historical facts open to ordinary investigation. These facts relate essentially to the man Jesus, his presentation of himself as God in human flesh, and his resurrection from the dead as proof of His deity.

---

[49]Kai Nielsen, "Can Faith Validate God-Talk?" in *New Theology No. 1*, eds. Martin E. Marty and Dean G. Peerman (New York: Macmillan, 1964), esp. p. 147; C.B. Martin, "A Religious Way of Knowing," in *New Essays in Philosophical Theology*, eds. Antony Flew and Alasdair MacIntyre (London: SCM Press, 1955), pp. 76–95; Frederick Ferre, *Language, Logic and God* (New York: Harper, 1961), pp. 94–104. See also philosopher John Hare's endeavor to rehabilitate Christian truth: "The Argument from Experience," in *Evidence for Faith: Deciding the God Question*, ed. John W. Montgomery, (Richardson: Probe Books, 1991).

## Paul on the Areopagus

Thus the rabbinic lawyer, Christian convert, and apostle—Paul of Tarsus—offered this gospel to Stoic philosophers at Athens as the historically verifiable fulfillment of natural religion and the natural law tradition, with their vague and insufficiently defined content.

> Some also of the Epicurean and Stoic philosophers met him [Paul at Athens]. And some said, "What would this babbler say?" Others said, "He seems to be a preacher of foreign divinities"—because he preached Jesus and the resurrection. And they took hold of him and brought him to the Areopagus, saying, "May we know what this new teaching is which you present?" . . . So Paul, standing in the middle of the Areopagus, said: "Men of Athens, I perceive that in every way you are very religious. For as I passed along, and observed the objects of your worship, I found also an altar with this inscription, 'To an unknown god.' What therefore you worship as unknown, this I proclaim to you . . . The times of ignorance God overlooked, but now he commands all men everywhere to repent, because he has fixed a day on which he will judge the world in righteousness by a man whom he has appointed, and of this he has given assurance to all men by raising him from the dead." (Acts 17:18–19, 22–23, 30–31)[50]

At one point in his speech, Paul asserted that human life is the product of divine creation, "as even some of your [Stoic] poets have said" (Acts 17:28), thereby making clear that classical natural law thinking was correct as far as it went, though it did not by any means go far enough.[51] Its completion could be found in Jesus, the

---

[50]The late classical scholar E.M. Blaiklock of the University of Auckland, New Zealand, in delivering the Annual Wheaton College Graduate School Lectures October 21–22, 1964, on the subject of Paul's Areopagus address, noted that Paul ignored the Epicureans ("the Sadducees of the Greeks"), doubtless because of the intellectual dishonesty into which their movement had fallen, and concentrated on the Stoics, who continued to hold a high view of natural law.

[51]In Acts 17:28 Paul quoted Cleanthes (300 B.C.), *Hymn to Zeus 5*, and/or Aratus (270 B.C.), *Phoenom 5*. Cf. J.B. Lightfoot's essay, "St. Paul and Seneca," in his *St. Paul's Epistle to the Philippians* (Grand Rapids: Zondervan, 1953); F.W. Farrar, *Seekers After God* (London: Macmillan, 1906); N.B. Stonehouse, *Paul Before the Areopagus, and Other New Testament Studies* (Grand Rapids: Eerdmans, 1957);

Man whom God ordained, and his divine character was verifiable through his resurrection from the dead.

## Why Legal Reasoning?

Elsewhere I have argued this case by employing standard, accepted techniques of historical analysis.[52] Here we shall use legal reasoning and the law of evidence. The advantage of a jurisprudential approach lies in the difficulty of jettisoning it: legal standards of evidence develop as essential means of resolving the most intractable disputes in society (dispute settlement by self-help—the only alternative to adjudication—will tear any society apart). Thus one cannot very well throw out legal reasoning merely because its application to Christianity results in a verdict for the Christian faith.[53]

Significantly, both in philosophy and in theology, there are moves to introduce juridical styles of reasoning. Stephen Toulmin, professor of philosophy at Leeds and one of the foremost analytical philosophers of our time, presents a veritable call to arms:

> To break the power of old models and analogies, we can provide ourselves with a new one. Logic is concerned with the soundness of the claims we make—with the solidity of the grounds we produce to support them, the firmness of the backing we provide for them—or, to change the metaphor, with the sort of case we present in defence of our claims. The legal analogy implied in this last way of putting the point can for once be a real help. So let us forget about psychology, sociology, technology and mathematics, ignore the echoes of structural engineering and collage in the words "grounds" and "backing," and take as our model the discipline of jurisprudence. Logic (we may say) is generalized jurisprudence. Arguments can be compared with

---

B. Gartner, *The Areopagus Speech and Natural Revelation* (Lund, 1955); and J. Sevenster, *Paul and Seneca* (Leiden: Brill, 1961).

[52]John Warwick Montgomery, "Jesus Christ and History," chapters 1–5 in this book.

[53]Cf. John Warwick Montgomery, "Legal Reasoning and Christian Apologetics," in his *The Law Above the Law*, (Minneapolis: Bethany, 1975), pp. 84–90; and idem, *Law and Gospel: A study in Jurisprudence* (Edmonton: Canadian Institute for Law, Theology and Public Policy, 1995), pp. 34–37.

lawsuits, and the claims we make and argue for in extra-legal contexts with claims made in the courts, while the cases we present in making good each kind of claim can be compared with each other.[54]

Mortimer Adler, at the end of his careful discussion of the question of God's existence, employs, not the traditional philosophical ideal of Cartesian absolute certainty, but the legal standards of proof by preponderance of evidence and proof beyond reasonable doubt:

> If I am able to say no more than that a preponderance of reasons favor believing that God exists, I can still say I have advanced reasonable grounds for that belief . . . I am persuaded that God exists, either beyond a reasonable doubt or by a preponderance of reasons in favor of that conclusion over reasons against it. I am, therefore, willing to terminate this inquiry with the statement that I have reasonable grounds for affirming God's existence.[55]

And from the jurisprudential side, Jerome Hall recognizes the potential for arbitrating central issues of religion and ethics by the sophisticated instrument of legal reasoning.

> Legal rules of evidence are reflections of "natural reason," and they could enter into dialogues in several ways, for example, to test the validity of theological arguments for the existence of God and to distinguish secular beliefs, even those held without any reasonable doubt, from faith that is so firm (Job's) that it excludes the slightest shadow of doubt and persists even in the face of evidence that on rational grounds is plainly contradictory. In these and other ways the rationality of the law of evidence in the trial of an issue of fact joins philosophical rationalism in raising pertinent questions about faith.[56]

---

[54]Stephen E. Toulmin, *The Uses of Argument* (Cambridge: Cambridge University Press, 1958), p. 7.

[55]Mortimer J. Adler, *How to Think About God* (New York: Macmillan, 1980), p. 150.

[56]Jerome Hall, "Religion, Law and Ethics—A Call for Dialogue," *Hastings Law Journal 29* (July 1978): p. 1273. We are not persuaded that Job's faith was quite as firm—or as irrational—as Hall suggests, but the reference to Job is in any case an *obiter dictum*!

## Four Key Questions

In terms of our discussion, what are the "pertinent questions about faith"? Four overarching questions need to be answered: (1) Are the historical records of Jesus solid enough to rely upon? (2) Is the testimony in these records concerning his life and ministry sufficiently reliable to know what he claimed about himself? (3) Do the accounts of his resurrection from the dead, offered as proof of his divine claims, in fact establish those claims? (4) If Jesus' deity is established in the foregoing manner, does he place a divine stamp of approval on the Bible so as to render its pronouncements apodictically certain? Let us see how legal reasoning helps to answer each of these key questions

Basic to any determination of the soundness of Christian claims is the question of the reliability of the pertinent historical documents. The documents at issue are not (*pace* the man on the Clapham omnibus) Josephus, Tacitus, Pliny the Younger, or other pagan references to Jesus, though these do of course exist. Such references are secondary at best, since none of these writers had firsthand contact with Jesus or with his disciples. The documents on which the case for Christianity depends are the New Testament writings, for they claim to have been written by eyewitnesses or by close associates of eyewitnesses (indeed, their origin in apostolic circles was the essential criterion for including them in the New Testament).

## New Testament Documents As Competent Evidence

How good are these New Testament records? They handsomely fulfill the historian's requirements of transmissional reliability (their texts have been transmitted accurately from the time of writing to our own day), internal reliability (they claim to be primary-source documents and ring true as such), and external reliability (their authorships and dates are backed up by such solid extrinsic testimony as that of the early 2nd century writer Papias, a student of John the Evangelist, who was told by him that the first three Gospels were indeed written by their traditional authors).[57] Harvard's

---

[57]Montgomery, "Jesus Christ and History"; F.F. Bruce, *The New Testament Documents: Are They Reliable?* (5th ed.; London: Inter-Varsity, 1960); John Warwick

Simon Greenleaf, the greatest 19th century authority on the law of evidence in the common-law world, applied to these records the "ancient documents" rule: Ancient documents will be received as competent evidence if they are "fair on their face" (i.e., offer no internal evidence of tampering) and have been maintained in "reasonable custody" (i.e., their preservation has been consistent with their content). He concluded that the competence of the New Testament documents would be established in any court of law.[58]

The speculation that the Gospel records were "faked" some three hundred years after the events described in them (a viewpoint gratuitously proffered by Professor Trevor-Roper) is dismissed by Lord Chancellor Hailsham, England's highest ranking legal luminary, with an apt lawyer's illustration.

> [What] renders the argument invalid is a fact about fakes of all kinds which I learned myself in the course of a case I did in which there was in question the authenticity of a painting purporting to be by, and to be signed by, Modigliani. This painting, as the result of my *Advice on Evidence*, was shown to be a fake by X-ray evidence. But in the course of my researches I was supplied by my instructing solicitor with a considerable bibliography concerning the nature of fakes of all kinds and how to detect them. There was one point made by the author of one of these books which is of direct relevance to the point I am discussing. Although fakes can often be made which confuse or actually deceive contemporaries of the faker, the experts, or even the not so expert, of a later age can invariably detect them, whether fraudulent or not, because the faker cannot fail to include stylistic or other material not obvious to contemporaries because they are contemporaries, but which stand out a mile to later observers because they reflect the

---

Montgomery, "The Fourth Gospel Yesterday and Today," in his *The Suicide of Christian Theology* (Minneapolis: Bethany, 1971), pp. 428–465. On the extra-biblical evidence, see C.R. Haines, *Heathen Contact with Christianity During Its First Century and a Half: Being All References to Christianity Recorded in Pagan Writings During That Period* (Cambridge: Deighton Bell, 1923); and Gary R. Habermas, *Ancient Evidence for the Life of Jesus* (Nashville: Tomas Nelson, 1984).

[58]Simon Greenleaf, The Testimony of the Evangelists, Examined by the Rules of Evidence Administered in Courts of Justice, reprinted in Montgomery, The Law Above the Law, pp. 91 ff.

standards, or the materials, or the styles of a succeeding age to that of the author whose work is being faked.[59]

As for the skepticism of the so-called higher critics (or redaction critics) in the liberal theological tradition, it stems from an outmoded methodology (almost universally discarded today by classical and literary scholars and by specialists in comparative Near Eastern studies), and from unjustified philosophical presuppositions (such as anti-supernaturalistic bias and bias in favor of religious evolution).[60] A.N. Sherwin-White, a specialist in Roman law, countered such critics in his 1960–61 Sarum Lectures at the University of London.

> It is astonishing that while Graeco-Roman historians have been growing in confidence, the twentieth century study of the Gospel narratives, starting from the no less promising material, has taken so gloomy a turn in the development of form-criticism that the more advanced exponents of it apparently maintain—so far as an amateur can understand the matter—that the historical Christ is unknowable and the history of His mission cannot be written. This seems very curious when one compares the case for the best-known contemporary of Christ, who like Christ is a well-documented figure—Tiberius Caesar. The story of his reign is known from four sources, the *Annals* of Tacitus and the biography of Suetonius, written some eighty or ninety years later, the brief contemporary record of Velleius Paterculus, and the third century history of Cassius Dio. These disagree amongst themselves in the wildest possible fashion, both in major matters of political action or motive and in specific details of minor events. Everyone would admit that Tacitus is the best of all the

---

[59]Lord Hailsham (Quintin Hogg), *The Door Wherein I Went* (London: Collins, 1975), pp. 32–33; the theological and apologetic portion of Lord Hailsham's autobiography has been photolithographically reproduced in *The Simon Greenleaf Law Review 4* (1984–85), pp. 1–67, with editorial introduction by John Warwick Montgomery.

[60]C.S. Lewis, "Modern Theology and Biblical Criticism," in his *Christian Reflections* (Grand Rapids: Eerdmans, 1967), pp. 152–166; Gerhard Maier, *The End of the Historical-Critical Method*, trans. E.W. Leverenz and R.F. Norden (St. Louis: Concordia, 1977); and cf. John Warwick Montgomery, "Why Has God Incarnate Suddenly Become Mythical?" in *Perspectives on Evangelical Theology*, eds. Kenneth S. Kantzer and Stanley N. Gundry (Grand Rapids: Baker Book House, 1979), pp. 57–65.

sources, and yet no serious modern historian would accept at face value the majority of the statements of Tacitus about the motives of Tiberius. But this does not prevent the belief that the material of Tacitus can be used to write a history of Tiberius.[61]

The conclusion is inescapable: If one compares the New Testament documents with universally accepted secular writings of antiquity, the New Testament is more than vindicated. Some years ago, when I debated philosophy professor Avrum Stroll of the University of British Columbia on this point,[62] he responded: "All right. I'll throw out my knowledge of the classical world." At which the chairman of the classics department cried: "Good Lord, Avrum, not that!"

## The Testimonial Question

If, as we have seen, the New Testament records are sound historical documents, how good is their testimony of Jesus? This is a question of great importance, since the accounts tell us plainly that Jesus claimed to be nothing less than God-in-the-flesh, come to earth to reveal God's will for the human race and to save human beings from the penalty of their sins. Moreover, the same testimony meticulously records Jesus' post-resurrection appearances, so a decision as to its reliability will also bear directly on our third major question, the historicity of the resurrection.

In a court of law, admissible testimony is considered truthful unless impeached or otherwise rendered doubtful. This is in accord with ordinary life, where only the paranoiac goes about with the bias that everyone is lying. (Think of Cousin Elmo, convinced that he is followed by Albanians.) The burden, then, is on those who would show that the New Testament testimony to Jesus is not worthy of belief. Let us place the Gospel testimony to Jesus under the legal microscope to see if its reliability can be impeached.

---

[61]A.N. Sherwin-White, *Roman Society and Roman Law in the New Testament* (Oxford: Clarendon Press, 1963), p. 187.

[62]My lectures and Professor Stroll's are chapters 1–5 and Appendix "A" in this book.

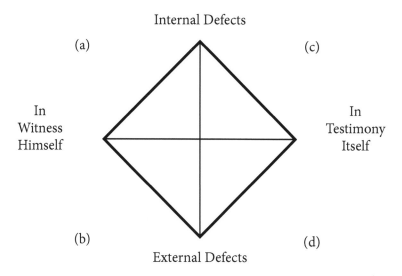

**Figure 1.**  A Construct for Exposing Perjury

Here we employ a construct for attacking perjury that has been labeled "the finest work on that subject."[63] McCloskey and Schoenberg offer a fourfold test for exposing perjury, involving a determination of internal and external defects in the witness himself on the one hand and in the testimony itself on the other.[64] We can translate their schema into diagrammatic form thusly:

## Internal Defects in the Witnesses?

(a) Internal defects in the witness himself refer to any personal characteristics or past history tending to show that the "witness is inherently untrustworthy, unreliable, or undependable." Were the apostolic witnesses to Jesus persons who may be disbelieved because they were "not the type of persons who can be trusted"? Did they have criminal records or is there reason to think they were pathological liars? If

---

[63]Alan Saltzman, "Criminal Law: How to expose Perjury Through Cross-Examination," *Los Angeles Daily Journal*, November 4, 1982.

[64]Patrick L. McCloskey and Ronald L. Schoenberg, *Criminal Law Advocacy* (New York: Matthew Bender, 1984), vol. 5, para. 12.01 [b].

anything, their simple literalness and directness is almost painful. They seem singularly poor candidates for a James Bond thriller or for being cast in the role of "Spy and Counterspy." But perhaps they were *mythomanes*—people incapable of distinguishing fact from fantasy? They themselves declare precisely the contrary: "We did not follow cleverly devised myths [Gk. *mythoi*, 'myths'] when we made known to you the power and coming of our Lord Jesus Christ, but we were eyewitnesses of his majesty." (2 Peter 1:16)[65]

## External Motives to Falsify?

(b) But perhaps the apostolic witnesses suffered from external defects, that is, "motives to falsify"?

> Not all perjurers have committed prior immoral acts or prior crimes. Frequently, law abiding citizens whose pasts are without blemish will commit perjury, not because they are inherently unworthy, but because some specific present reason compels them to do so in the case at bar. Motive, then, becomes the common denominator. There is a motive for every act of perjury. The second major way in which the cross-examiner can seek to expose perjury, therefore, is to isolate the specific motive which causes the witness to commit perjury.[66]

Surely no sensible person would argue that the apostolic witnesses would have lied about Jesus for monetary gain or as a result of societal pressure. To the contrary: They lost the possibility both of worldly wealth and of social acceptability among their Jewish peers because of their commitment to Jesus.[67] Might that very affection for and attachment to Jesus serve as a motive to falsify?

---

[65]2 Peter 1:16. In vv. 17–18, Peter states expressly that he was with Jesus when he was transfigured. (Matthew 17:2; Mark 9:2; Luke 9:29).

[66]McCloskey and Schoenberg, *Criminal Law Advocacy*, vol. 5, para. 12.03.

[67]A point made as early as the fourth century by the historian Eusebius of Caesarea, and reiterated by such classical apologists as Hugo Grotius ("the father of international law"), in "The Resurrection of Christ proved from credible testimony," in his *The Truth of the Christian Religion*, trans. John Clarke (new ed.; London; William Baynes, 1825), bk. 2, sec 6, pp. 85–88; this section of Grotius' work

Not when we remember that their master expressly taught them that lying was of the devil.[68]

## Internal Defects in the Testimony?

(c) Turning now to the testimony itself, we must ask if the New Testament writings are internally inconsistent or self-contradictory. Certainly, the Four Gospels do not give identical, verbatim accounts of the words or acts of Jesus. If they did, that fact alone would make them highly suspect, for it would point to collusion.[69] The Gospel records view the life and ministry of Jesus from four different perspectives— just as veridical witnesses to the same accident will present different but complementary accounts of the same event. If the objection is raised that the same occurrence or pericope is sometimes found at different times or places in Jesus' ministry, depending upon which Gospel one consults, the simple answer is that no one Gospel contains or was ever intended to contain the complete account of Jesus' three-year ministry.[70] Furthermore, Jesus (like any preacher) certainly spoke the same messages to different groups at different times. And suppose he did throw the money-changers out of the Temple twice: is it not strange, in light of their activity and his principles, that he only threw them out twice? (We would have expected it every Saturday—Sabbath—night.) Observe also how honestly and in what an unflattering manner the apostolic company picture themselves in these records. Mark, Peter's companion, describes him as having a consistent case of foot-in-the-mouth disease; and the Apostles

---

is photolithographically reproduced in John Warwick Montgomery, ed., *Jurisprudence: A Book of Readings*, (Strasbourg; International Scholarly Publishers, 1980), pp. 327–330.

[68]John 8:44, etc.

[69]"People just do not see things in an identical way when their positions and chances for observation vary. [If so,] the case is a frame up." F. Lee Bailey and Henry B. Rothblatt, *Fundamentals of Criminal Advocacy* (San Francisco: Bancroft-Whitney, 1974), para. 500, p. 240.

[70]John 20:30–31; 21:25. See Edmund H. Bennett, *The Four Gospels from a Lawyer's Standpoint* (Boston; Houghton, Mifflin, 1899); photolithographically reproduced with editorial introduction by John Warwick Montgomery in *The Simon Greeleaf Law Review 1* (1981–82).

in general are presented (in Jesus' own words) as "slow of heart to believe all that the prophets have spoken" (Luke 24:25). To use New Testament translator J.B. Phillips' expression, the internal content of the New Testament records has the "ring of truth."[71]

*External Defects in the Testimony?*

(d) Finally, what about external defects in the testimony itself, i.e., inconsistencies between the New Testament accounts and what we know to be the case from archaeology or extra-biblical historical records? Far from avoiding contact with secular history, the New Testament is replete with explicit references to secular personages, places, and events. Unlike typical sacred literature, myth, and fairytale ("Once upon a time . . ."), the Gospel story begins with, "In those days a decree went out from Caesar Augustus that all the world should be enrolled" (Luke 2:1).[72] Typical of the New Testament accounts are passages such as the following:

> In the fifteenth year of the reign of Tiberius Caesar, Pontius Pilate being governor of Judea, and Herod being tetrarch of Galilee, and his brother Philip tetrarch of the region of Ituraea and Trachonitis, and Lysanias tetrarch of Abilene, in the high priesthood of Annas and Caiaphas, the word of God came to John the son of Zechariah in the wilderness; and he went into all the region about Jordan, preaching a baptism of repentance for the forgiveness of sins. (Luke 3:1–3)

Modern archaeological research has confirmed again and again the reliability of New Testament geography, chronology, and general history.[73] To take but a single, striking example: After the rise of liberal biblical criticism, doubt was expressed as to the historicity of Pontius Pilate, since he is mentioned even by pagan historians only

---

[71]J.B. Phillips, *Ring of Truth: A Translator's Testimony* (New York; Macmillan, 1967).

[72]See John Warwick Montgomery, *Myth, Allegory and Gospel* (Edmonton: Canadian Institute for Law, Theology and Public Policy, 2000), pp. 11–31, 116–118.

[73]See, for example, E.M. Blaiklock, *The Archaeology of the New Testament* (Grand Rapids: Zondervan, 1970); and Edwin M. Yamauchi, *The Stones and the Scriptures* (Grand Rapids: Baker Book House, 1981).

in connection with Jesus' death. Then, in 1961, came the discovery at Caesarea of the now famous "Pilate inscription," definitely showing that, as usual, the New Testament writers were engaged in accurate historiography.

Thus on no one of the four elements of the McCloskey-Schoenberg construct for attacking perjury can the New Testament witnesses to Jesus be impugned.

## The Complexities of Deception

Furthermore, one should realize (and non-lawyers seldom do realize) how difficult it is to succeed in effective lying or misrepresentation when a cross-examiner is at work. Richard A. Givens, in his standard work, *Advocacy*, in the McGraw-Hill Trial Practice Series, diagrams ordinary truthful communication and then contrasts it with the tremendous complexities of deceitful communication (Figures 2 and 3).[74]

Observe that the witness engaged in deception must, as it were, juggle at least three balls simultaneously, while continually estimating his chances of discovery: he must be sure he doesn't say anything that contradicts what his examiner knows (or what he thinks his examiner knows); he must tell a consistent lie ("liars must have good memories"); and he must take care that nothing he says can be checked against contradictory external data. Givens' point is that successful deception is terribly difficult, for the psychological strain and energy expended in attempting it makes the deceiver exceedingly vulnerable.

> The wider the angles of divergence between these various images, the more confusing the problem, and the more "higher mathematics" must be done in order to attempt to avoid direct conflicts between these elements. The greater the angle of deception employed, the greater the complexity and the lower the effectiveness of these internal mental operations. If this is conscious, we attribute this to lying. If it is unconscious, we lay it to the "bias" of the witness.

---

[74]Richard A. Givens, *Advocacy* (New York: McGraw-Hill, 1980), pp. 13–14.

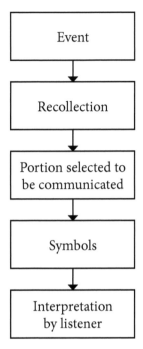

**Figure 2.**   The Mental Process in "Simple", i.e., Truthful Communications

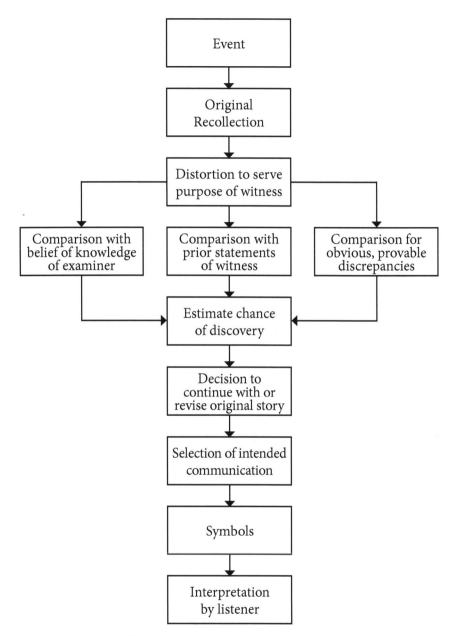

**Figure 3.** The Lying Witness

If one is lying or strongly biased, it is not enough to simply dredge up whatever mental trace there may be of the event and attempt to articulate it in answer to a question. Instead, all of the various elements mentioned must be weighed, a decision made as to the best approach, a reply contrived that is expected to be most convincing, and then an effort made to launch this communication into the minds of the audience.

The person with a wide angle of divergence between what is recalled and the impression sought to be given is thus at an almost helpless disadvantage, especially if confronting a cross-examiner who understands the predicament.

If the audience includes both a cross-examiner and a tribunal, the number of elements to be considered becomes even greater. The mental gymnastics required rise in geometric proportion to the number of elements involved.[75]

Now, wholly apart from the question as to whether the New Testament witnesses to Jesus were the kind of people to engage in such deception (and we have already seen, in examining them for possible internal and external defects, that they were not): had they attempted such a massive deception, could they have gotten away with it? Admittedly, they were never put on a literal witness stand, but they concentrated their preaching on synagogue audiences. This put their testimony at the mercy of the hostile Jewish religious leadership who had had intimate contact with Jesus' ministry and had been chiefly instrumental in ending it.

## Hostile Witnesses as *De Facto* Cross-Examiners

Such an audience eminently satisfies Givens' description of "both a cross-examiner and a tribunal": They had the means, motive, and opportunity to expose the apostolic witness as inaccurate and deceptive if it had been such. The fact that they did not can only be effectively explained on the ground that they could not. It would seem, for example, inconceivable that the Jewish religious leadership, with their intimate knowledge of the Old Testament, would have sat idly by as

---

[75]Ibid, p. 12.

the Apostles proclaimed that Jesus' life and ministry had fulfilled dozens of highly specific Old Testament prophecies (birth at Bethlehem, virgin birth, flight to Egypt, triumphal entry, sold by a friend for thirty pieces of silver, etc., etc.), had that not been true. Professor F.F. Bruce of the University of Manchester underscores this fundamental point as to the evidential significance of the hostile witnesses:

> It was not only friendly eyewitnesses that the early preachers had to reckon with; there were others less well disposed who were also conversant with the main facts of the ministry and death of Jesus. The disciples could not afford to risk inaccuracies (not to speak of willful manipulation of the facts), which would at once be exposed by those who would be only too glad to do so. On the contrary, one of the strong points in the original apostolic preaching is the confident appeal to the knowledge of the hearers; they not only said, "We are witnesses of these things," but also, "As you yourselves also know" (Acts 2:22). Had there been any tendency to depart from the facts in any material respect, the possible presence of hostile witnesses in the audience would have served as a further corrective.[76]

## Insanity?

We do not waste time on the possibility that the disciples were suffering from insane delusions. First, because the law presumes a man sane, and there is no suggestion in the accounts that the Apostles were otherwise. Second, because the point Professor Bruce has just stressed concerning the hostile witnesses applies with equal force to the insanity suggestion: had the disciples distorted Jesus' biography for any reason, including a deluded state of mind, the hostile witnesses would surely have used this against them.

## The Hearsay Rule

The functional equivalence of hostile witnesses with formal cross-examination goes far to answer the occasionally voiced objection

---

[76]Bruce, *New Testament Documents*, pp. 45–46.

that the apostolic testimony to Jesus would be rejected by a modern court as "hearsay," i.e., out-of-court statements tendered to prove the truth of their contents. Let us note at the outset the most severe problem with hearsay testimony: the originator of it is not in Court and so cannot be subjected to searching cross-examination.

Thus even when New Testament testimony to Jesus would technically fall under the axe of the hearsay rule, the hostile witnesses as functional cross-examiners reduce the problem to the vanishing point.

In the second place, the hearsay rule exists in Anglo-American common law (no such rule is a part of the Continental civil law tradition) especially as a technical device to protect juries from secondhand evidence. Following the virtual abolition of the civil jury in England, the Civil Evidence Act of 1968 in effect eliminated the hearsay rule by statute from civil trials—on the ground that judges can presumably sift even second-hand testimony for its truth-value.[77] In the United States, and in English criminal trials, the exceptions to the hearsay rule have almost swallowed up the rule, and one of these exceptions is the "ancient documents" rule (to which we referred earlier), by which the New Testament documents would indeed be received as competent evidence.

To be sure, the underlying principle of the hearsay rule remains vital: that a witness ought to testify "of his own knowledge or observation," not on the basis of what has come to him indirectly from others. And the New Testament writers continually tell us that they are setting forth that "which we have heard; which we have seen with our eyes, which we have looked upon and touched with our hands . . . the word of life" (1 John 1:1).

## A Challenge to the Reader

Simon Greenleaf's summation of the testimonial case for Jesus' life, ministry, and claims about himself offers a perennial challenge to the earnest seeker for truth.

---

[77]Peter Murphy, *A Practical Approach to Evidence* (London: Financial Training, 1982), pp. 23–24; cf. George B. Johnston, "The Development of Civil Trial by Jury in England and the United States," *Simon Greenleaf Law Review* 4 (1984–85): pp. 69–92.

All that Christianity asks of men on this subject is that they would be consistent with themselves; that they would treat its evidences as they treat the evidence of other things; and that they would try and judge its actors and witnesses as they deal with their fellow men, when testifying to human affairs and actions, in human tribunals. Let the witnesses be compared with themselves, with each other, and with surrounding facts and circumstances; and let their testimony be sifted, as if it were given in a court of justice, on the side of the adverse party, the witness being subjected to a rigorous cross-examination. The result, it is confidently believed, will be an undoubting conviction of their integrity, ability, and truth. In the course of such an examination, the undesigned coincidences will multiply upon us at every step in our progress; the probability of the veracity of the witnesses and of the reality of the occurrences which they relate will increase, until it acquires, for all practical purposes, the value and force of demonstration.[78]

## The Question of the Resurrection

At the heart of the apostolic testimony and proclamation is the alleged resurrection of Jesus Christ from the dead. During his ministry, Jesus offered his forthcoming resurrection as the decisive proof of his claim to deity.[79]

Did the resurrection in fact occur?[80]

---

[78]Greenleaf, *Testimony of the Evangelists*, pp. 132–133.

[79]Matthew 12:38–40; 16:4; Luke 11:29; John 2:18–22.

[80]I.e., did the resurrection occur in ordinary history? We do not deal here with the unverifiable vagaries of "hyper-history" or "supra-history" (as in the thought of Karl Barth and certain of his neo-orthodox followers), or with "existential" resurrections (Rudolf Bultmann and the post-Bultmannians). I have discussed elsewhere these modern theological attempts to have one's cake and eat it too: John Warwick Montgomery, "Karl Barth and Contemporary Theology of History," in his *Where is History Going?*, pp.100–117; cf. idem, "Luther's Hermeneutic vs. the New Hermeneutic," in his *In Defense of Martin Luther* (Milwaukee: Northwestern Publishing House, 1970), pp. 40–85.

*Testimonial Evidence, Not Metaphysics, the Key*

First, consider the written records of the resurrection and of detailed post-resurrection appearances which occurred over a forty-day period.[81] What is important here is that these accounts are all contained in the very New Testament documents whose historical reliability we have already confirmed and are testified to by the same apostolic witnesses whose veracity we have just established. To do an abrupt *volte-face* and now declare those documents and witnesses to be untrustworthy because they assert that Jesus rose from the dead would be to substitute a dubious metaphysic ("resurrections from the dead are cosmically impossible"—and how does one establish that in a relativistic, Einsteinian universe?) for careful historical investigation. We must not make the mistake of 18th century philosopher David Hume, who thought he could avoid evidential drudgery by deductively reasoning from the gratuitous premise that "a firm and unalterable experience has established the laws of nature" to the (entirely circular) conclusions: "there must be a uniform experience against every miraculous event" and "that a dead man should come to life has never been observed in any age or country."[82]

*The Missing Body*

Second, we should reflect upon the force of the "missing body" argument of Frank Morison,[83] who was converted to Christianity through his investigation of the evidence for the resurrection. His argument proceeds as follows: (1) If Jesus didn't rise, someone must have stolen the body; (2) the only people involved were the Roman

---

[81]Concerning the historical and evidential value of these appearances, see Merrill C. Tenney, *The Reality of the Resurrection* (New York: Harper. 1963); Josh McDowell, *The Resurrection Factor* (San Bernardino: Here's Life Publishers, 1981); Richard Riss, *The Evidence for the Resurrection of Jesus Christ* (Minneapolis: Bethany, 1977); and Sir Norman Anderson, *The Evidence for the Resurrection* (London: Inter-Varsity, 1966).

[82]David Hume, "Of Miracles," in his *An Enquiry Concerning Human Understanding* (1748); for critique, see C.S. Lewis, *Miracles* (New York: Macmillan, 1947), esp. chaps. 8 and 13; and John Warwick Montgomery, *The Shape of the Past* (rev. ed.; Minneapolis: Bethany, 1975), pp. 289–293.

[83]Frank Morison, *Who Moved the Stone?* (London: Faber & Faber, 1944).

authorities, the Jewish religious leaders, and Jesus' disciples; (3) the Romans and the Jewish religious leaders would certainly not have taken the body, since to do so would have been against their own interests (the Romans wanted to keep Palestine quiet and the Jews wanted to preserve their religious influence);[84] and (4) the disciples would hardly have stolen the body and then died for what they knew to be untrue; (5) ergo—by process of elimination—Jesus rose from the dead just as the firsthand accounts declare.

I have shown elsewhere that Antony Flew's attempt to avoid the impact of this argument is unsuccessful.[85] When Flew says that Christians simply prefer a biological miracle (the resurrection) to a psychological miracle (the disciples dying for what they knew to be false), he completely misses the point. The issue is not metaphysical preference; it is testimonial evidence. No such evidence exists to support a picture of psychologically aberrant disciples, while tremendously powerful testimonial evidence exists to the effect that Jesus physically rose from the dead.

During the last few years, more inventive attempts to explain away the resurrection have appeared. Schonfield's *Passover Plot* argues that Jesus induced his own crucifixion, drugging himself so as to survive just long enough in the tomb to convince the fuddled disciples that he had risen.[86] (*Quaere*: How does this square with Jesus' own moral teachings? And does it not leave us with precisely the same problem as to what finally happened to the body?) Von Daniken—who turned to pseudo-scientific writing while serving a prison sentence in Switzerland for embezzlement, fraud, and forgery[87]—"explains" the resurrection by

---

[84]Cf Matthew 27:62–66.

[85]John Warwick Montgomery, "Science, Theology, and the Miraculous," in his *Faith Founded on Fact* (Edmonton: Canadian Institute for Law, Theology and Public Policy, 1978, 2001), pp. 43–73, esp. p.54.

[86]See Edwin M. Yamauchi, "Passover Plot or Easter Triumph? A Critical Review of H. Schonfield's Recent Theory," in John Warwick Montgomery ed., *Christianity for the Tough Minded* (Edmonton: Canadian Institute for Law, Theology and Public Policy, 1973, 2001), pp. 261–271.

[87]Von Daniken had "obtained the money [over $130,000 in debts] by misrepresentation of his financial situation, falsifying the hotel's books to make it appear solvent. A court psychiatrist examined von Daniken and found him a prestige

suggesting that it was the product of a close encounter of the third kind: Jesus was a kind of Martian cleverly dressed in a Jesus suit who knew a few tricks such as how to appear to rise from the dead.

## Legal Reasoning Is Probabilistic

Aren't such hypotheses possible? Doubtless, in our contingent universe, anything is possible (as one philosopher said) except squeezing toothpaste back into the tube. But legal reasoning operates on probabilities, not possibilities: preponderance of evidence in most civil actions; evidence beyond reasonable (not beyond all) doubt in criminal matters.[88] The *Federal Rules of Evidence* defines relevant evidence as "evidence having any tendency to make the existence of any fact that is of consequence to the determination of the action more probable or less probable than it would be without the evidence."[89] Suppose a jury brought in a verdict of "innocent" because it is always possible that invisible Martians, not the accused, were responsible for the crime! Judges in the United States carefully instruct juries to pay attention only to the evidence in the case, and to render verdicts in accord with it. A guilty verdict in a criminal matter should be rendered only if the jury cannot find any reasonable explanation of the crime (i.e., any explanation in accord with the evidence) other than that the accused did it. May we suggest that the tone and value of discussions about Jesus' resurrection would be considerably elevated if equally rigorous thinking were applied thereto?

Can we base ultimates (Jesus' deity, a commitment to him for time and eternity) on mere probabilities? The analytical philosophers have shown that we have no other choice: only formal ("analytic") truths (e.g., the propositions of deductive logic and of pure

seeker, a liar and an unstable and criminal psychopath with an hysterical character, yet fully accountable for his acts." (Richard R. Lingerman, "Erich von Daniken's Genesis," *New York Times Book Review*, March 31, 1974, p. 6.)

[88]Probability reasoning is virtually universal in the law; it operates both in common law and in non-common law systems of jurisprudence, and in "civilized" and "primitive" legal systems indiscriminately. See Montgomery, *Law and Gospel*, pp. 35–36.

[89]*Federal Rules of Evidence*, p. 401. This definition was derived from Professor James Bradley Thayer's classic *Preliminary Treatise on Evidence* (1898).

mathematics) can be demonstrated absolutely—and the absoluteness here is due to the definitional nature of their axiomatic foundations, as with Euclid's geometry. All matters of fact ("synthetic" assertions) are limited to probabilistic confirmation, but this does not immobilize us in daily life. We still put our very lives in jeopardy every day on the basis of probability judgments (crossing the street, consuming packaged foods and drugs, flying in airplanes, etc.). And the law in every land redistributes property and takes away liberty (if not life) by verdicts and judgments rooted in the examination of evidence and probabilistic standards of proof.

## What Weight of Evidence?

But the issue here is a miracle: a resurrection. How much evidence ought a reasonable man require in order to establish such a fact? Could evidence ever justify accepting it? Thomas Sherlock, Master of the Temple Church (owned by two of the four guilds of English barristers, the Honourable Societies of the Inner and Middle Temple) and Bishop of London, well answered these questions in the 18th century:

> Suppose you saw a Man publickly executed, his Body afterwards wounded by the Executioner, and carry'd and laid in the Grave; that after this you shou'd be told, that the Man was come to Life again: What wou'd you suspect in this Case? Not that the Man had never been dead; for that you saw yourself: But you wou'd suspect whether he was now alive. But wou'd you say, this Case excluded all human Testimony; and that Men could not possibly discern, whether one with whom they convers'd familiarly, was alive or no? Upon what Ground cou'd you say this? A Man rising from the Grave is an Object of Sense, and can give the same Evidence of his being alive, as any other Man in the World can give. So that a Resurrection consider'd only as a Fact to be proved by Evidence, is a plain Case; it requires no greater Ability in the Witnesses, than that they be able to distinguish between a Man dead, and a Man alive: A Point, in which I believe every Man living thinks himself a Judge.[90]

---

[90]Thomas Sherlock, *The Tryal of the Witnesses of the Resurrection of Jesus* (London: J. Roberts, 1729), p. 62; Sherlock's book is photolithographically reproduced in Montgomery, *Jurisprudence.*

Bishop Sherlock is certainly correct that a resurrection does not in principle create any insuperable evidential difficulty. Phenomenally (and this is all we need worry about for evidential purposes) a resurrection can be regarded as death followed by life,

D, then L.

Normally, the sequence is reversed, thus:

L, then D.

We are well acquainted with the phenomenal meaning of the constituent factors (though we do not understand the "secret" of life or why death must occur). Furthermore, we have no difficulty in establishing evidential criteria to place a person in one category rather than in the other. Thus the eating of fish[91] is sufficient to classify the eater among the living, and a crucifixion is enough to place the crucified among the dead. In Jesus' case, the sequential order is reversed, but that has no epistemological bearing on the weight of evidence required to establish death or life. And if Jesus was dead at point A, and alive again at point B, then resurrection has occurred: *res ipsa loquitur*.[92]

## How Reliable Are Eyewitnesses?

However, does not the unreliability of eyewitness testimony cast doubt on an event as extraordinary as the resurrection? Psychologists such as Loftus have pointed up genuine dangers in eyewitness testimony.[93] Nonetheless, as we have already seen, it remains the cornerstone of legal evidence. As for the reliability of identifying

---

[91]See Luke 24:36–43.

[92]I have applied proof by *res ipsa loquitur* to the resurrection in my *Law & Gospel*, p. 35.

[93]Elizabeth F. Loftus, *Eyewitness Testimony* (Cambridge: Harvard University Press, 1979); cf. her popular article on this subject in *Psychology Today* 18, no. 2 (February 1984): pp. 22–26.

acquaintances (the precise issue in the disciples' post-resurrection identifications of Jesus), specialists on the subject agree that "the better acquainted a witness is with a subject, the more likely it is that the witness' identification will be accurate." These same authorities add that "in an eyewitness context, the greatest challenge to the advocate's power of persuasion is presented by the attempt to argue, without support from expert testimony, the unreliability of an unimpeached eyewitness's identification of a prior acquaintance."[94] And this is precisely what we have in the case under consideration: disciples like Thomas provide "unimpeached eyewitness identification" of the resurrected Jesus with whom they had had the most intimate acquaintance for the immediately preceding three-year period.[95] No advocate's "power of persuasion" is going to make a difference to that kind of identification evidence.

## Facts and Interpretation

Finally, the objection may be offered: even granting Jesus' resurrection, is that fact alone enough to establish his deity and the truth of his claims? Theological presuppositionalists Carl F.H. Henry and Ronald H. Nash tell us that there are no self-interpreting facts,[96] and Calvinists R.C. Sproul and John Gerstner, as well as evangelical

---

[94]Edward B. Arnolds *et al.*, *Eyewitness Testimony: Strategies and Tactics* (New York: McGraw-Hill, 1984), pp. 400–401.

[95]John 20:19–28.

[96]Carl F.H. Henry, *God, Revelation and Authority* (Waco, Tex.: Word Books, 1976), vol. 1, pp. 220–223, 230–238, 256–263; vol. 2, pp. 313–334; Ronald H. Nash, "The Use and Abuse of History in Christian Apologetics," *Christian Scholar's Review* 1, no. 3 (Spring 1971), pp. 217–226; Ronald H. Nash, *Christian Faith and Historical Understanding*, (2d ed.; Dallas: Probe Books, 1989). I have responded to Carl Henry in Montgomery, *Faith Founded on Fact*, pp. xvii–xxv. Paul D. Feinberg wrote a devastating critique of Nash's "Use and Abuse of History" in "History: Public or Private? A Defense of John Warwick Montgomery's Philosophy of History," *Christian Scholar's Review* 1, no. 4 (Summer 1971), pp. 325–331; it is reprinted in Montgomery, *Shape of the Past*, pp. 375–382. Nash's book, *Christian Faith and Historical Understanding* (which, sadly, does not seem to have benefited in any way from Feinberg's insights), has been critically reviewed by Francis J. Beckwith, "Does Evidence Matter?" *Simon Greenleaf Law Review* 4 (1984–85), pp. 231–235.

neo-Thomist Norman L. Geisler, insist that an independent theistic structure must be established to make any theological sense out of Jesus' resurrection.[97] We profoundly disagree. Even Rat—famous for his leading role in Kenneth Grahame's *The Wind in the Willows*, but hardly an accomplished epistemologist—becomes exasperated with his companion for not recognizing that facts can be self-interpreting:

> "Do-you-mean-to-say," cried the excited Rat, "that this doormat doesn't tell you anything?"
>
> "Really, Rat" said the Mole quite pettishly, "I think we've had enough of this folly. Who ever heard of a doormat telling anyone anything? They simply don't do it. They are not that sort at all. Doormats know their place."
>
> "Now look here, you—you thick-headed beast," replied the Rat, really angry, "this must stop. Not another word, but scrape—scrape and scratch and dig and hunt round, especially on the sides of the hummocks, if you want to sleep dry and warm tonight, for it's our last chance?"

Elsewhere we have argued in detail that facts—historical and otherwise—"in themselves provide adequate criteria for choosing among variant interpretations of them."[98] Philosopher Paul D. Feinberg has defended that case with inexorable logic:

> Let us consider an example from recent history. It can be substantiated that some 6 million Jews died under German rule in the Second World War. Let me suggest two mutually exclusive interpretations. First, these events may be interpreted as the actions of a mad man who was insanely anti-Semitic. The deaths were murders, atrocities. Second, it might be asserted that Hitler really loved the Jews. He had a deep and abiding belief in heaven and life after death. After reviewing Jewish history, Hitler decided that the Jews had been persecuted enough, and

---

[97]R.C. Sproul, John Gerstner, and Arthur Lindsley, *Classical Apologetics* (Grand Rapids: Zondervan, 1984); Norman L. Geisler, *Miracles and Modern Thought*, with a response by R.C. Sproul (Dallas: Probe Books, 1982).

[98]John Warwick Montgomery, "Gordon Clark's Historical Philosophy." In Montgomery, *Where Is History Going?*, esp. p. 164.

because of his love for them he was seeking to help them enter eternal blessedness. If no necessity exists between events and interpretation, then there is no way of determining which meaning is correct. We would never be justified in claiming that one holding the latter view is wrong. This is both repugnant and absurd. There must be an empirical necessity that unites an event or fact with its correct interpretation.[99]

Beyond this, we merely remind the reader that the very nature of legal argument (judgments rendered on the basis of factual verdicts) rests on the ability of facts to speak for themselves. As a single illustration, taking the leading U.S. Supreme Court case of *Williams v. North Carolina* (the "second Williams case"), which stands for the proposition that a divorce on substituted or constructive service in one state need only be given full faith and credit by another state when the parties have acquired a *bona fide* domicile in the divorcing state. In the course of its opinion, the Court declared:

> Petitioners, long time residents of North Carolina, came to Nevada, where they stayed in an auto-court for transients, filed suits for divorce as soon as the Nevada law permitted, married one another as soon as the divorces were obtained, and promptly returned to North Carolina to live. It cannot reasonably be claimed that one set of inferences rather than another regarding the acquisition by petitioners of new domicils [sic] in Nevada could be drawn from the circumstances attending their Nevada divorces.[100]

## Two Reasons to Accept the Deity of Jesus

Geisler misrepresents us when he says that we hold that "the resurrection is so bizarre, so odd, that only a supernatural explanation will adequately account for it."[101] In our view there are two compelling reasons to accept Jesus' resurrection as implicating his deity.

---

[99]Feinberg, "History: Public or Private?" p. 379.

[100]*Williams v. North Carolina*, 325 U.S. 226, 65 Sup. Ct. 1092, 157 A.L.P. 1366.

[101]Geisler, *Miracles and Modern Thought*, p. 66. Remarkably, Geisler seems entirely unacquainted with my detailed treatment of this issue in my book *Faith Founded on Fact*, pp. 43–73, even though my book was published four years before his.

First, "this miracle deals effectively with the most fundamental area of man's universal need, the conquest of death"[102]—a truth recognized in law by the "dying declaration" exception to the hearsay rule (even the declaration of the homicide victim without religious faith is admissible in evidence, on the ground that one is particularly likely to tell the truth when conscious of the immanence of that most terrible of existential events).[103] If death is indeed that significant, then "not to worship one who gives you the gift of eternal life is hopelessly to misread what the gift tells you about the Giver."[104]

In the second place, there are logically only two possible kinds of explanation or interpretation of the fact of the resurrection: that given by the person raised, and that given by someone else. Surely, if only Jesus was raised, he is in a far better position (indeed, in the only position!) to interpret or explain it. Until Von Daniken, for example, rises from the dead, we will prefer Jesus' account of what happened. And Jesus tells us that his miraculous ministry is explicable because he is no less than God in human form: "I and my Father are one"; "He who has seen me has seen the Father."[105] Theism then becomes the proper inference from Jesus' resurrection as he himself explained it—not a prior metaphysical hurdle to jump in order to arrive at the proper historical and evidential interpretation of that event.

## Jesus Places his Stamp of Approval on the Bible

Jesus' deity in itself establishes the truth of the Christian message, over against competing religions and secular worldviews. And Jesus' teachings *per se*, being God's teachings, represent an infallible guide to human life and conduct. But Jesus does more even than this. By his direct statements concerning the Old Testament as divine revelation[106] and by his consistent quoting of it as trustworthy and

---

[102]Ibid, p. 61.

[103]See, for example, *State v. Elliott*, 45 Iowa 486.

[104]Montgomery, *Faith Founded on Fact*, p. 61.

[105]John 10:30; 14:8–9, slightly paraphrased; cf. Mark 2:5–7; 14:61–64.

[106]E.g., Matthew 4:4; 5:17–19; John 5:39; 10:35.

divinely authoritative in all respects,[107] Jesus put upon it his (i.e., God's) *imprimatur*. By giving his Apostles a special gift of the Holy Spirit to recall infallibly what he had taught them,[108] and, by implication, to recognize apostolicity in others, he proleptically stamped with approval as divine revelation the future writings of Apostles (the original twelve, minus Judas Iscariot, plus Paul—grafted in as Apostle to the Gentiles)[109] and writings by their associates (Mark, Luke, etc.) whose accuracy the Apostles were in a position to verify. As a result, the entire Bible—Old Testament and New—becomes an unerring source of absolute principles.[110]

## Two Objections to the Foregoing Argument

Two objections may be raised to the argument we have just presented. First, why should the mere fact that God says something guarantee its truth? Second, what if the incarnate Christ was so limited to the human ideas of his time that his stamp of approval on the Bible represents no guarantee of its absolute accuracy?

The first of these arguments is reflected in Descartes' discussion of God as a possible "Evil Genius"—a cosmic liar. But if he were, he would be a divine and, therefore, consummate liar, so you would be incapable of catching him at it. In short, he would be a better liar than you are a detective. So the very idea of God-as-liar is meaningless—an analytically unverifiable notion in principle. Once you have met God incarnate, you have no choice but to trust him as to the way of salvation and as to the reliability of the entire Bible.

---

[107]For example, Matthew 12:38–42; 19:3–6; 24:37–39; Luke 24:25–27.

[108]John 14:26; 16:12–15. Swiss theologian Oscar Cullman has made much of the apostolic memory as the inspired link between Jesus' ministry and the New Testament scriptures.

[109]Acts 1:21–26; 9:26–27; Galatians 2:11–13; 2 Peter 3:15–16.

[110]John Warwick Montgomery ed., *God's Inerrant Word: An International Symposium on the Trustworthiness of Scripture* (Minneapolis: Bethany, 1974); idem, *Crisis in Lutheran Theology*, (2nd ed.; Minneapolis: Bethany, 1973); idem, *Shape of the Past*, pp. 139–145.

The suggestion that Jesus was limited to human and fallible ideas (the so-called Kenotic theory[111] of liberal theology) also collapses under its own weight. On Kenotic reasoning, either Jesus chose to conform his statements to the fallible ideas of his time (in which case he was an opportunist who, in the spirit of Lenin, committed one of the most basic of all moral errors, that of allowing the end to justify the means);[112] or he couldn't avoid self-limitation in the very process of incarnation (in which case incarnation is of little or no value to us, since there is then no guarantee that it reveals anything conclusive). And note that if such a dubious incarnation mixed absolute wheat with culturally relative chaff, we would have no sufficient criterion for separating them anyway, so the "absolute" portion would do us no good!

## Jesus, God's Son, Has Spoken

To meet man's desperate need for apodictic principles of human conduct, an incarnate God must not speak with a forked tongue. And, as we have seen, no divine stuttering has occurred. To the contrary, his message can be relied upon as evidentially established, a sure light shining in a dark world, illuminating the path to eternity.

---

[111]From the Greek noun *kenosis*, whose verb form ("empty oneself / divest oneself of privileges") is applied to Christ in Philippians 2:6–8. However, biblical teaching on incarnation has no resemblance to the liberal theological theory of Jesus' fallibility. Theological liberals—typically—developed the theory to have their cake (a divine Jesus) and eat it too (simultaneous rejection of Jesus' conservative view of scriptural authority). Cf. Montgomery, *Crisis in Lutheran Theology*, pp. 91–93. It is perhaps worth noting that the well-known passage in the Gospels in which Jesus states that he does not know the hour of his Second Coming (Mark 13:32) is no confirmation of Kenotic theory, for (1) only a single, eschatological item of knowledge is involved, and (2) Jesus' disclaimer of knowledge on this point shows that in his incarnate state he was nonetheless fully aware of the boundaries of his knowledge, and being in control of his knowledge he would not have advertently or inadvertently given false or misleading information when he did make positive assertions (e.g., on the reliability of the Bible).

[112]John Warwick Montgomery, *The Marxist Approach to Human Rights: Analysis and Critique* (Edmonton: Canadian Institute for Law, Theology and Public Policy, in press), pp. 51–53, 138–141.

# Appendices

# Appendix A
# "Did Jesus Really Exist?"

*By Avrum Stroll*

Before beginning today's talk, I should like to discuss a matter with you which seems to me of great urgency and importance. And I should like to introduce what I have to say about this subject by reading the concluding paragraphs of a letter printed in the "Letters to the Editor" column of the *Vancouver Sun* last Friday. This letter, signed with the name "Mrs. Ruth D. Golman," contains a lengthy and highly critical discussion of an address given before the Philosophy Club a week ago today by Professor Peter Remnant of the Philosophy Department. Its concluding paragraphs read as follows:

> A man's religion is his own personal right and privilege, with which no other being has the right to interfere. Therefore, Dr. Remnant also has the right to his own personal views on the matter of God. But the University of British Columbia is, or should be, a purely educational institution. As a citizen of British Columbia, and a taxpayer, I therefore strongly protest his action in using the university and his affiliation therewith as the medium through which to express his personal ideas on religion by means of a lecture to over a thousand students. Not only are such views obnoxious to the time of the year, but to the time of world history. Never has mankind needed the consciousness of divine wisdom and strength as much as now.

There would be no point or purpose in reading this letter to you if it were simply an isolated expression of misinformation about the nature and function of a university in a democratic society. But unfortunately this is not the case. The views expressed by the writer echo a chorus of voices raised in condemnation of the university ever since the Cuban crisis. It is time that the character of this challenge be identified, be recognized for what it is, and that the sort of claims it makes be met head-on and resisted. If we fail to do so, we not only abandon one role of the teacher—to explain what he is about, and why his activities constitute important civic functions—but we also, by our inaction, open the door to further attacks on the democratic process itself.

For what we have here in Mrs. Golman's letter (and in the letters like it) is a direct challenge to the right of a professor, or for that matter, anyone else, to speak his mind before a group of university students. Mrs. Golman not only disagrees with Dr. Remnant's philosophical position—and we surely wish to defend, and even insist upon, her right to do so—but with his right to express it, using, as she puts it, the university facilities to do so. This is a clear and unmistakable challenge to academic freedom.

But the challenge does not end here: it is this further threat to freedom of inquiry in the university which I wish to stress at this gathering. Dr. Remnant addressed this club at the invitation of its executive; the professors who spoke to a student group about the Cuban situation did so at the invitation of the executive of that group. What is being challenged here, in effect, is the right of student groups in a free university in a democratic society to invite speakers of their choice to address them.

What I wish to insist on today is that it is the defining function of a university in a democratic society to provide a forum where free debate and free inquiry can take place. It is not only the right, but indeed the duty, of faculty members and students to consider, examine, judge and make appraisals of the issues which concern them. This right can only be exercised in those circumstances where there are no barriers to free inquiry. The university is, in this respect, a model or smaller image of the wider democratic community itself. The university student exposes himself to a wide variety of opinions, views, and doctrines on the assumption that the techniques and procedures he develops in the process of making such judgments will be carried on into his daily activities as a citizen of the community when he leaves the university. It is a condition of being a good citizen in a democratic community that one treat the issues which come before him in this way, and it is important to stress that it is the university which provides part of the training ground for his becoming a good citizen in this sense.

The voices which speak with Mrs. Golman are in effect threatening us with censorship, with some restriction upon the right of faculty members and students to inquire into the subjects of their interests in an effort to develop mature, responsible and informed views of the world. This threat must not go unanswered. I urge you here today to protest against this challenge to your right to freedom of inquiry and investigation. How you go about doing this, I leave to you. But speak out. As the long history of tyranny only too well teaches us: if we do not speak out under such conditions, we may ultimately lose the right to speak out at all.

As a philosopher speaking (by invitation I might add) to the members of this philosophical association, may I use this opportunity for purposes of instruction? Let us not forget the best argument which has been proposed against the imposition of censorship. Roughly speaking, it is this: one of the paradoxes involved in the notion of censorship itself is that it cannot be applied to all members of a society. Even Plato, history's most celebrated defender of the need for censorship, wished only to apply it to the masses of his ideal society, but not to the ruling classes.

And why? Because he correctly saw that those who are required to make wise and judicious laws for society must expose themselves to all the facts, to full and open debate about them, to all the pros and cons of a question which untrammeled investigation could produce. He saw clearly that without a free inquiry of this sort all the facts could not come under the surveillance of those responsible for making just laws; and so he argued, correctly I believe, that they should be exempted from censorship. In a democratic society, which is a self-governing institution, it is the citizen who participates in the governing process and who is, in the end, responsible for the laws which bind the members of the body politic. By the reasons I have just advanced, it follows that there can be no censorship in a democratic society: that all of its citizens must be in a position through free and unhampered inquiry to assess the merits of a question by having access to all the facts and opinions concerning it. As a training ground for the discovery and appraisal of facts the university is thus at the core of the democratic, decision-making process itself.

Let us now turn, if I may employ a Gilbertian phrase, from matters political to matters theological. And here I wish to discuss the question, "Did Jesus of Nazareth really exist?" This question, "Did Jesus exist?", is to be distinguished from the question, "Did Christ exist?" I will illustrate why later on. I might also point out that in distinguishing these questions from one another, I do not mean to revive any variant of the Monophysite heresy, a heresy which turned on the question whether Jesus was fully human or fully divine, or to what degree he was both.

What I want to do, instead, may be summarized as follows. In contemporary philosophical theology one of the most widely debated questions concerns the relation between the historical Jesus, a man supposedly living in Palestine sometime between 9 B.C. and A.D. 32, and the Jesus described in the Gospel writings. The form this discussion takes is reminiscent of the discussion which historians of ancient philosophy have engaged in concerning the existence of Socrates. "Did Socrates really exist?" Some scholars, Winspear for example, have argued "No." Most historians of the period have rejected this view, and have argued that he did. But the evidence for his existence is fragmentary. It mainly consists of a report by Xenophon of the trial of Socrates, allusions to a certain Socrates in two of the plays of Aristophanes, and the writings of Plato which purport to contain an eyewitness account of the life and activities of Socrates. But even if it is granted that there was such a person, it is difficult to separate the views of the real Socrates from those of Plato, and all sorts of conjectures about the relation between the views of Socrates and those of Plato have been put forth in recent years. A typical and characteristic response of many philosophers who are not historians is to raise the question: "What difference does it make whether there was a real Socrates or not? The figure who appears in the Platonic dialogues, even if only a literary invention, represents a certain philosophical position on all sorts of important matters: on the nature of knowledge, or the relation between knowledge and virtue, and so forth—and it is these positions which are, and ought to be, of interest to the contemporary philosopher."

I find it of some interest that a comparable issue should exist in contemporary theology about the nature of the historical Jesus and his relation to the figure portrayed in the gospels. This issue is the main theme which runs through Albert Schweitzer's book, *The Quest of the Historical Jesus*, first published *[in English]* in 1910. In concluding this work, Schweitzer says: "There is nothing more negative than the result of the critical study of the life of Jesus. The Jesus of Nazareth who came forward publicly as the Messiah, who preached the ethic of the Kingdom of God, who founded the Kingdom of Heaven upon earth, and died to give his work its final consecration, never had any existence. He is a figure designed by rationalism, endowed with life by liberalism, and clothed by modern theology in an historical garb." (p. 398). And again, in developing this theme, he remarks: "Jesus means something to our world because a mighty spiritual force streams forth from him and flows through our time also. This fact can neither be shaken nor confirmed by any historical discovery. It is the solid foundation of Christianity. The mistake was to suppose that Jesus could come to mean more to our time by entering into it as a man like ourselves. That is not possible. First because such a Jesus never existed." (p. 399)

One of the most important Christian theologians of the postwar period is Rudolf Bultmann, whose work evidences a remarkable lack of concern with the historical Jesus. Expressing what has been described as "a mixture of radical historical skepticism and existentialist disinterest in objective history" (Schubert M. Ogden), Bultmann, from the time of his 1926 monograph on Jesus to his lecture given before the Heidelberg Academy of the Sciences in 1959, takes the view that there is a difference in principle between the historical Jesus and the message of the church that sets an impassible limit to any attempt to establish their identity. Insofar as the old quest for the historical Jesus sought and seeks to reconstruct a picture of the life and personality of the historical Jesus and in that way to provide historical justification for the existential decision of faith, Bultmann completely rejects the question. In his view, such an effort is historically impossible and theologically illegitimate. The knowledge available to us, he argues, through responsible critical analysis of the Synoptic Gospels simply is insufficient for the reconstruction of a picture of Jesus' character and inner development.

This view has, of course, had its critics among New Testament scholars, among them James Robinson in his *A New Quest of the Historical Jesus*, published in 1959, Gunter Bornkamm (a pupil of Bultmann's) in his *Jesus of Nazareth*, and Schubert M. Ogden (see his article, "Bultmann and the New Quest," in the July 1962 issue of the *Journal of Bible and Religion*). Now I do not wish to take part in this controversy; not only am I not a theologian and hence not competent to form judgments on this matter, but the issues which turn on detailed considerations are simply too complex to be discussed in such a meeting as this one.

What I should like to do, though, is to raise the question: "What evidence is there for the existence of the historical Jesus?" without in any way attempting to relate this evidence to the figure presented in the gospels.

I should begin by pointing out that the number of modern, or even relatively modern, scholars who explicitly deny the existence of Jesus is few indeed. The orthodox position, which is one of caution, is expressed by Bornkamm who says, writing in 1956:

> . . . admittedly the difficulties in the way of arriving at a reasonably assured historical knowledge in the field of tradition about Jesus have increased. That is inherent in the nature of the sources . . . their investigation has, in point of fact, greatly enriched our understanding, but at the same time has made our knowledge of the historical Jesus ever more uncertain. It has also driven the ship of enquiry so far in another direction that the map of the actual history of Jesus, once so clearly marked, must in the opinion of many today be in all honesty left blank.

But there do exist even stronger views than these, although they are expressed by a minority of scholars. Bruno Bauer's work, especially his *Criticism of the Gospel History of the Synoptics*, written in 1841, contains an explicit denial of the existence of Jesus. Toynbee notes that the suggestion by Frazer that the Jesus legend may have risen from annual rites celebrating the death of a mock king cannot be entirely discounted, while Robertson and P.L. Couchoud are both modern proponents of the purely legendary origin of Jesus. But the weight of scholarly opinion is against these writers, and in his *From the Stone Age to Christianity*, first published in 1946, William Foxwell Albright, biblical archeologist at Johns Hopkins, dismisses Couchoud's work as containing "historical extravagances."

One may, I think not unfairly, summarize the scholarly opinion on this question as follows: the existence of Jesus is beyond question, but the information we have about him is a composite of fact and legend which cannot reliably be untangled.

Given that this is the situation, what I should like to do here today, then, is to examine the evidence which is often adduced in favor of the view that Jesus did exist. It seems to me that a review of the available evidence will be of some interest to you. I find it tenuous; more tenuous, indeed than do the scholars I have quoted, but nonetheless, for reasons which I shall advance in connection with recent findings involving the Dead Sea Scrolls, I also find it persuasive that there was an historical Jesus. This is a matter I shall turn to after considering the evidence in detail.

The first question which strikes anyone who approaches the question of the existence of Jesus is whether there is any first hand evidence for his existence; for example, documents written by eye-witnesses to his ministry.

Our possible sources of such direct evidence fall into three classes: the writings of Roman historians of the first century A.D.; the writings of Jewish historians such as Philo and Josephus Flavius; and the writings from Christian sources.

The works of Seneca, Petronius, Pliny the Elder, Juvenal, Martial, Quintilian, Epictetus, Plutarch, Appian and Philo, written in the first century, make no reference to Jesus or even to the existence of Christianity, a fact which has weighed heavily with some scholars when they discuss the question of possible interpolations by later writers into the works of Josephus, the Jewish historian. Gibbon, for example, in his *History of the Decline and Fall of the Roman Empire* (written during the late 18th century) ironically comments on this fact as follows:

> During the age of Christ, of his apostles and of their first disciples, the doctrine which they preached was confirmed by innumerable

prodigies. The lame walked, the blind saw, the sick were healed, the dead were raised, demons were expelled, and the laws of Nature were frequently suspended for the benefit of the church. But the sages of Greece and Rome turned aside from the awful spectacle, and pursuing the ordinary occupations of life and study, appeared unconscious of any alteration in the moral or physical government of the world.

The case of Pliny is of particular interest in this connection. According to Christian tradition, the whole earth, or at least Palestine, was covered with darkness for three hours after the death of Jesus. This took place within the life of the elder Pliny, who has a special chapter in his *Natural History* on the subject of eclipses, but he says nothing of this eclipse (see Gibbon, Chapter XV, Vol. ii, pp. 69–70).

The first mention of Jesus by a Roman historian occurs in Tacitus' *Annals* written in A.D. 117, or about 85 years after the death of Jesus. Tacitus says (Fifteenth Book, Chapter 44), speaking about the burning of Rome under Nero in A.D. 64:

In order to counteract the report which laid the blame for this conflagration on Nero he accused persons who were called Christians (by the people) and who were hated for their misdeeds of the guilt, and visited the most excruciating penalties upon them. He from whom they had taken their name, Christ, had been executed in the reign of Tiberius by the Procurator Pontius Pilate; but though this superstition was thus for a moment put down, it arose again not only in Judea, the original home of this plague, but even in Rome itself, in which city every outrage and every shame finds a home and wide dissemination. First a few were seized who confessed, and then on their denunciation a great number of others, who were not, however, accused of the crime of incendiarism, but of that of hating humanity. Their execution was made a public amusement; they were covered with the skins of wild beasts and then torn by dogs or crucified or prepared for the pyre, and then burned as soon as night came, to illuminate the city. For this spectacle Nero lent his gardens and he even arranged circus games in which he mingled with the people in the costume of a charioteer, or mounted a racing chariot. Although these men were criminals deserving of the severest punishment, there was some public sympathy for them, as it seemed they were being sacrificed not to the general weal, but to the cruelty of a single man.

Scholars have disagreed about the weight to be attached to this passage. The contemporary Roman historians do not mention the Christians in connection with the burning of Rome, and Dio Cassius writing a century after Tacitus does not mention them either. It is worth noting that the name "Jesus" is not mentioned; and as I shall point out later, the fact that these people are called Christians is also not regarded as particularly significant. The words "*ho christos*" are simply the Greek equivalents of the Hebrew term, *Mashiah*, or Messiah: and in a period of Messianic fervor it is quite likely that many individuals were declaring themselves to be the Messiah, come to fulfill the prophetic claims advanced in the Old Testament. Homer Smith in *Man and His Gods* (p. 179) commenting on this passage says:

> Some historians have debated whether this passage is wholly authentic, or contains Christian interpolations; but the answer is relatively unimportant since at this late date Tacitus could have obtained the all-important name of Pontius Pilate from Christian tradition.

The earliest mention of Jesus by a non-Christian is to be found in Josephus Flavius' *Antiquities*, a work written in A.D. 94–95 or some 15 years after his *History of the Jewish Wars*. In Chapter 3 of the eighteenth book of this work, Josephus says:

> About this time there lived Jesus, a wise man, if he may be named a man, for he achieved miracles and was a teacher of men, who gladly accepted his truth, and found many adherents among Jews and Hellenes. This man was the Christ. Although Pilate then had him crucified on the accusation of the most excellent men of our people, those who had first loved him remained faithful to him nevertheless. For on the third day he appeared to them again, arisen to a new life, as God's prophets had prophesied this and thousands of other miraculous things of him. From him the Christians take their name; their sect has since then not ceased.

In Chapter 9 of the twentieth book, Josephus again speaks of Jesus, saying that the High Priest Ananus, under the rule of the Governor Albinus (in the time of Nero) had succeeded in having "James, the brother of Jesus, the so-called Christ, haled to court, together with a number of others, indicted as transgressors of the law and stoned."

Josephus, who was born approximately in 37, could not have been an eyewitness to the events reported; and, in view of the fact that he was an Orthodox Jew, a Pharisee who had no particular reason to color the facts in favor of the Christians, these passages have long been suspect as interpolations into his works by later Christian writers. Shurer, in his *History of the Jewish people during the Time of Jesus Christ*, published in 1901, argues that the first passage I have cited was added in the third century by a Christian copyist who was evidently offended by the failure of Josephus to produce any information concerning the person of Jesus while he repeats the most childish gossip from Palestine; and Karl Kautsky adds in 1907, that it is certain that the passage is a forgery and not written by Josephus at all. Origen who lived from A.D. 185–254 mentions in his commentary on Matthew that it is peculiar that Josephus did not believe in Jesus as the Christ, given that he refers to James as Christ's brother. Scholarly examination of the evidence surrounding this matter indicates that the second passage is also, in all probability, an interpolation by a Christian writer sometime in the second century. The problem raised by this passage, however, is too detailed for examination here.

These passages from Josephus, and the passage from Tacitus, contain the only information we have about the existence of Christ from non-Christian sources in the first century. It is clear that neither writer could have been an eyewitness to the events he describes, and that considered as indirect evidence for the existence of Jesus, none of the three passages will bear much weight.

The remaining evidence we possess which might possibly contain first-hand information about the existence of Jesus comes from Christian sources. This evidence itself falls into two classes, the Gospels according to Matthew, Mark, Luke and John forming one of the categories, the writings of St. Paul forming the other main category. Let us turn to the Gospels first.

The Gospels, of course, purport to contain descriptions of the life and activities of Christ, from the time of his nativity, through his baptism, crucifixion and resurrection. Until the attention of historical scholarship was directed to these documents early in the nineteenth century, it was commonly assumed that they contained eyewitness reports of the events described. This assumption was questioned later in the century by D.F. Strauss in his *Leben Jesu* (1835), by Reimarus, Bauer and others. The issue which was debated by these scholars turned upon the dating of the documents in question, members of the Tubingen School, for example, dating the Gospel according to St. John as late as A.D 140. This led to a distinction between the Gospels—a distinction first noted by Origen. It was pointed out that the Gospels of Mark, Matthew and Luke formed a unit: that similar phrases, a similar arrangement of the narrative, takes place within them. Placing these Gospels side by side, one can correlate passage with passage for large sections of the discourse they contain. Hence they were called the Synoptic Gospels in contradistinction to the Johannine Gospel. K. Lachmann in 1835 also suggested that the Gospel according to St. Mark was the oldest of these documents, and that many of the common features exhibited by the Gospels of Luke and Matthew were derived from the Marcion gospel. This general result is still accepted, although the dispute about the dating of the Gospels still continues. C.H. Roberts in 1935 published a fragment of the Gospel according to John which dates from the early part of the 2nd century, and which showed that the Gospel in question cannot have been written much later than A.D. 100. But even accepting this date, it is unlikely that the author of John could have been an eyewitness to the events he describes. Even this is disputed by C.C. Torrey who argues that all the Gospels are translations into Greek of works originally composed in Aramaic and that none of the Gospels dates from the period later than A.D. 70. But in general, New Testament scholars have been hesitant to accept this result and contend instead that Mark was written about the time of the Fall of Jerusalem in A.D. 70, and that Matthew and Luke were probably composed between A.D. 70 and 90, with the Gospel according to John being composed shortly thereafter.

The issues involving the dating of the Gospels are extremely complex. According to many New Testament scholars even the document we now have called the Gospel according to St. Mark is antedated by an older document originally written by Matthew, one of the twelve disciples, and commonly called the "Q" document. The existence of this document is inferred primarily from the fact that the Gospels of Luke and Matthew contain in common large sections of the teaching of Jesus not borrowed from Mark or from one another, and therefore presumably derived from some other common source. This document called "Q," it is argued, for example by C.J. Cadoux, was originally written in Aramaic, and was subsequently translated into Greek. If it does contain the testimony of a personal disciple of Jesus its date may be very early and its reliability may be very great. Unfortunately, there is no direct evidence for the existence of this document, the only evidence being an inference from the large amounts of common material found in Luke and in Matthew.

In recent years, though, the question whether the documents we have in the Gospels were actually composed by eyewitnesses to the activities of Christ has been relegated to a position of secondary importance. For internal reasons it is extremely unlikely that the writers of the documents we possess would have been eyewitnesses to the activities of Jesus. C.J. Cadoux, late professor of Church History at Mansfield College in Oxford, describes the situation in the following words: (because of time I shall read his comments only about the Gospel of Matthew pp. 14–15).

> The Gospel which bears the name of "Matthew" probably owes its designation to the fact that it incorporates Q (which it seems the real Matthew did write), but that, unlike the Gospel of Luke, the name of its final compiler had been forgotten. The compiler produced it in Greek, probably at or near Antioch in Syria in the eighties. He took Mark's Gospel as his framework. Into this he sandwiched large sections of Q, rearranging them in topical order, and also numerous passages from yet another supposed collection of material (usually called "M") which was strongly Jewish and even anti-Pauline in tone. It has been plausibly suggested, though there is no means of proving it, that the compiler desired to bridge the gulf between the Judaistic Jacob of Jerusalem and Paul the Apostle of the Gentiles, not only by utilizing these various sources, but by placing Peter in the position of the chief of the Apostles. Where "Matthew" (so I propose to designate this anonymous evangelist) is quoting Q or—as in the parables of the Treasure and the Pearldrawing on some other obviously trustworthy source, his authority stands high. But a close examination of the treatment he gives to his borrowings from Mark show that he allowed himself great 'freedom in editing and embroidering his material in the interest of what he regarded as the rightful honouring of the great Master. The same tendencies are often visible elsewhere

when he is reproducing Q or providing matter peculiar to himself. Anything, therefore, strictly peculiar to "Matthew" can be accepted as historical only with great caution.

But independently of these difficulties, even if there were reason to believe some of the material to express eyewitness accounts of Jesus' life, the accretion of legend, the description of miracles performed by Jesus, which exist in these writings make it difficult, if not impossible, to extract from them any reliable historical testimony about the events described. It is this fact which has led to the views of Dibelius, Schweitzer and Bultmann to the effect that the questions of the historical reliability of the picture of Christ given us in the gospels ought not to be the basis for the Christian tradition which stems from the gospels.

The last source which I wish to consider is St. Paul. We have thirteen epistles which are attributed to St. Paul, and all of them have at one time or other been challenged as genuine. But even independently of challenges of this sort, it is agreed that Paul never met Jesus, although he does claim personally in A.D. 68 to have met one of Jesus' contemporaries—his brother Jacob, also known as James. Paul also speaks of having persecuted "Christians" before his conversion experience—his seeing of Christ in a vision while on the road to Damascus.

In the foregoing account, then, I believe that I have summarized all the available evidence from writers of the first century A.D.—evidence which seems to me, in the light of this account, to be tenuous indeed.

In view of this is it then likely that the Jesus of the Gospels did not exist at all? I do not think that this conjecture is a likely one, and I shall now proceed to explain why.

This explanation will turn upon the history of Judaism after the destruction of the Temple in 586 B.C. From this period on, the Jews of Palestine lived in a power vacuum between the great powers of Egypt on the one side, and between Babylon, Persia on the other. The lives of Jewish citizens from this time until the beginning of the Christian period were insecure indeed. After the eclipse of Persia as a power, the Mediterranean world was conquered by the Greeks under Alexander, who regarded the Jews as barbarians and who insisted upon Hellenizing them. With the fall of Alexander, the Jews came under the domination of the Persian Seleucids, and then the Romans, both of whom initiated legislation inimical to the religious traditions of the Jews. The history of this period, as revealed by recent studies, exhibits a picture of a people living under the domination of foreign rulers, but unable to throw them off. Under such conditions, when revolution fails and all other alternatives are exhausted, the appeal of consolative religion, especially of another worldly sort, becomes very compelling. These frustrations produced documents such as the Book of Daniel of the O.T. and hundreds of apocryphal works written in the 1st and 2nd centuries B.C., documents of a species called "eschatological" and "apocalyptic" by Biblical scholars. They stress the coming of a Messiah or Redeemer who will throw off the hated conquerors, restore the law, bring about an era of peace. These documents clearly reveal the character of the post- exilic, pre-Christian era. It is difficult for us today—except in contemplating the consequences of nuclear war—to imagine what the temper of the time must have been like. With Judgment Day at hand, with the Kingdom of God momentarily expected, with the Messiah awaited, the intellectual ferment and the psychological instability produced by such expectations must have been tremendous. These expectations were reinforced by the writing of apocryphal works containing predictions of just these events to come. Not all the Jews accepted such apocalyptic teachings: the Sadducees, for example, rejected some of them, and they were in other respects inconsistent with the main teachings of Orthodox Judaism. Splinter groups formed, breaking away from these main areas of traditional Judaism, to go off into the wilderness there to await the coming of the Messiah, the Anointed One, the Christ. It is clear that the Essenes formed one such group. Indeed, it is believed that John the Baptist emerges from an Essene community preaching his doctrine that the Kingdom of God is at hand. It is also clear that recent investigations into the history of the period, aided by findings based on the Dead Sea Scrolls, indicate that the Essenes formed a much larger group within the Jewish community than had previously been believed. The belief in a coming apocalypse must thus have been part of the everyday views of a large segment of the Jews of the period.

Recent findings also reveal that persons whose lives and careers are strikingly parallel to that of the Christ as he is portrayed in the gospels—persons who practiced baptism, who defied the laws of the Pharisees, who were crucified and who even advanced a redemptive doctrine of salvation—were identified with the Messiah, or with the so-called King of the Jews, by the Essenes (see Matthew Black's *The Scrolls and Christian Origins*, 1961). There can be no doubt that this messianic fever was characteristic of the age, not only in the sense that the Messiah was awaited or expected momentarily, but more than that, there can be no doubt that some of the Jews contended, as early as the 2nd century B.C., that the Messiah had in fact arrived. Many contemporary scholars now believe that the origins of Christianity are to be located in the activities of these splinter, eschatologically dominated groups—and that the Pauline teaching that Jesus is the arrived Christ exhibits the influence of this group upon St. Paul. Paul's own reference to his previous persecution of Christians (i.e., of followers of the Messiah) bears this out, as does the gospel warning in Matthew that we must be aware of false christs, of false messiahs.

Given these facts, it seems to me likely that during this period a prophet arose, belonging to one of the apocalyptically minded Jewish sects, such as the Essenes, and that he did preach the doctrine that the Kingdom of God was at hand, that he did preach the soteriological doctrine that through his coming death mankind would be saved (it is in this sense that I believe one can justify or support the claim that the historical Jesus lived); but an accretion of legends grew up about this figure, was incorporated into the Gospels by various devotees of the movement, was rapidly spread throughout the Mediterranean world by the ministry of St. Paul; and that because this is so, it is impossible to separate these legendary elements in the purported descriptions of Jesus from those which in fact were true of him.

# Appendix B
# Letter from Edwin M. Yamauchi

Sir:

I would like to express my appreciation for your article, "History and Christianity." I am in agreement with your basic arguments, but would like to offer some comments.

The citation of Kenyon stressing the "textual advantage of the New Testament documents over *all other ancient manuscripts*" (italics mine) needs qualification. The writer is stressing the shortness of the interval between the composition of the N.T. books and our earliest extant manuscripts. This is, however, not unique. From ancient Mesopotamia we have the original autographs of a number of texts inscribed in stone or clay, e.g., the Harran inscriptions of Nabonidus. In N.T. times we have possibly the autographs, or at any rate early copies, of writings from the Qumran community. We have many originals or duplicates of letters from all periods, such as the Lachish letters, the Amarna letters, etc. The Qur'an of Muhammad was collated within a generation of the Prophet's death with relatively few variants.

The writer may have been thinking of Greek and Latin literary texts, most of which have come to us from medieval copies. Even here we have papyri representing half of the text of the *Odyssey* dating from as early as the 3rd century B.C.; the composition of the Odyssey is generally placed in the 8th century B.C.

With these qualifications, we must admit that the quantity and the antiquity of the manuscript evidence for the N.T are impressive. Kurt Aland from the *Institut fur Textforschung* in Munster, speaking in New York last month, pointed out that we now have 5,000 Greek manuscripts of the N.T and N.T. portions. The writer cited

Robertson, who in 1925 spoke of 4,000 Greek manuscripts. Westcott and Hort who provided a definitive edition of the Greek N.T. before the turn of the century had only 1,500 Greek texts available to them. Very significant has been the increase of papyri from the 4th, 3rd, and even 2nd centuries A.D. Before 1900 only 5 papyri had been published; we now know of 78 papyri.

I would agree with your stricture of Bultmann. Bultmann has attempted to demythologize the N.T. on the basis of a pre-Christian Gnostic myth, which he has constructed from late sources. On the one hand, the Coptic Gnostic codices from Nag-Hammadi in Egypt (1946) call for a radical revision of Bultmann's Gnostic construct. On the other hand, the Dead Sea Scrolls from Qumran (1947) corroborate the 1st century, Palestinian origin of the Gospel of John. Bultmann's attempt to criticize the 1st century N.T. documents on the basis of much later sources is methodologically unreasonable.

Yours truly,
Edwin M. Yamauchi
Professor of History
Miami University
Oxford, Ohio

# Suggestions for Further Study

(Works in print at the time of publication of this book.)

* Items available from 1517. The Legacy Project (www.1517legacy .com).

## Historical Evidence

Dr. John Warwick Montgomery

* Montgomery, John Warwick, *A Christian Philosophy of History* (New Reformation Publications, 2001, 2013) [audio download]

* Montgomery, John Warwick ed., *Christianity for the Tough Minded* (New Reformation Publications, 1973, 2001, 2013) [book]

* Montgomery, John Warwick, *Christianity in a Corner* (New Reformation Publications, 1996, 2013) [audio download]

* Montgomery, John Warwick, *Christians in the Public Square: Law, Gospel & Public Policy* (New Reformation Publications, 1996, 2013). Includes his essays "The Reasonable Reality of the Resurrection," "Why Has God Incarnate Suddenly Become Mythical?," "Jesus Takes the Stand: An Argument to Support the Gospel Accounts," and "A Lawyer's Case for Christianity." [book]

* Montgomery, John Warwick, *Defending the Biblical Gospel* (New Reformation Publications, 1973, 2001, 2013) Includes PDF study guide. [audio and PDF download]

* Montgomery, John Warwick ed., *Evidence for Faith: Deciding the God Question* (New Reformation Publications, 1991, 2003, 2015) [book]

* Montgomery, John Warwick, *Faith Founded On Fact* (New Reformation Publications, 1978, 2001, 2015) [book]

* Montgomery, John Warwick ed., *God's Inerrant Word: An International Symposium on the Trustworthiness of Scripture* (New Reformation Publications, 1974, 2015) [book]

* Montgomery, John Warwick, *Defending the Gospel through the Centuries - A History of Christian Apologetics* (New Reformation Publications, 1999, 2013) Includes PDF study guide. [audio and PDF download]

* Montgomery, John Warwick, "Is Man His Own God?" in Montgomery, John Warwick ed., *Christianity for the Tough Minded* (New Reformation Publications, 1973, 2001, 2015) [book]

* Montgomery, John Warwick and Wells, G.A., *Jesus: What Evidence?* (New Reformation Publications, 1996, 2013) [audio download]

* Montgomery, John Warwick and Grabbe, Lester, *Jesus' Resurrection: What Historical Evidence?* (New Reformation Publications, 1996, 2013) [audio download]

* Montgomery, John Warwick ed., *Myth, Allegory and Gospel: An Interpretation of J.R.R. Tolkien, C.S. Lewis, G.K. Chesterton, Charles Williams* (New Reformation Publications, 1974, 2000, 2015) [book]

* Montgomery, John Warwick, "Science, Theology and the Miraculous," in Montgomery, John Warwick, *Faith Founded On Fact* (New Reformation Publications, 1978, 2001, 2015)

* Montgomery, John Warwick, *The Search for Absolutes: A Sherlockian Inquiry* (New Reformation Publications, 1996, 2013) [audio download]

* Montgomery, John Warwick, *Sensible Christianity* (New Reformation Publications, 1996, 2013) [audio download]

* Montgomery, John Warwick, *The Shape of the Past: An Introduction to Philosophical Historiography* (Wipf and Stock, 1962, 2008) [book]

\* Montgomery, John Warwick, *Tractatus Logico-Theologicus* (Wipf and Stock, 2013) [book]

\* Montgomery, John Warwick, *The Transcendent Holmes* (Calabash Press, 2000) [book]

\* Montgomery, John Warwick, *Where Is History Going?* (New Reformation Publications, 1972, 2015) [book]

*Other Writers*

Anderson, J.N.D., *The Evidence for the Resurrection* (Inter-Varsity Fellowship, 1966)

Anderson, J.N.D., *Jesus Christ: The Witness of History* (Inter-Varsity Press, 1969, 1985)

\* Babcock, James F., "The Resurrection—a Credibility Gap?" in Montgomery, John Warwick ed., *Christianity for the Tough Minded* (New Reformation Publications, 1973, 2001, 2015)

\* Barnes, E.J., "The Dependability and Value of the Extant Gospel Manuscripts," in Montgomery, John Warwick, *The Shape of the Past* (Wipf and Stock, 1962, 2008)

Blomberg, Craig, *The Historical Reliability of the Gospels* (IVP Academic, 2007)

Bruce, F.F., *The Defense of the Gospel in the New Testament* (Eerdmans, 1959, rev. 1977, 1981)

Bruce, F.F., *Jesus and Christian Origins Outside the New Testament* (Eerdmans, 1974)

Bruce, F.F., *The New Testament Documents: Are They Reliable?* (Eerdmans, 2003)

Bruce, F.F., "Are The New Testament Documents Still Reliable?" in Kantzer, K.S. ed., *Evangelical Roots* (Nelson, 1978)

Burridge, Richard A., *What Are the Gospels? A Comparison with Graeco-Roman Biography* (Cambridge University Press, 1992)

Craig, William Lane, *Assessing the New Testament Evidence for the Historicity of the Resurrection of Jesus* (Edwin Mellen, 1989)

Craig, William Lane, *Reasonable Faith* (Crossway Books, 1994)

Earman, John, *Hume's Abject Failure: The Argument Against Miracles* (Oxford University Press, 2000)

Habermas, Gary R., *The Historical Jesus: Ancient Evidence for the Life of Christ* (College Press, 1996)

Habermas, Gary R. and Geivett, R. Douglas, *In Defense of Miracles: A Comprehensive Case for God's Acting in History* (Inter-Varsity Press, 1997)

Lewis, C.S., *Miracles* (rev. ed.: Fontana, 1960)

Lewis, C.S., "Modern Theology and Biblical Criticism" in Lewis, C.S., *Christian Reflections* (Eerdmans, 1967)

Machen, J. Gresham, *The Virgin Birth of Christ* (Harper, 1930)

Masters, Donald C., *The Christian Idea of History* (Waterloo Lutheran University, 1962)

McDowell, Josh, *The New Evidence That Demands a Verdict* (Thomas Nelson, 1999)

Moreland, J.P. and Wilkins, Michael J., *Jesus Under Fire* (Zondervan, 1996)

Morison, Frank, *Who Moved the Stone?* (Faber & Faber, 1930)

* Newman, Robert C., "Miracles and the Historicity of the Easter Week Narratives," in Montgomery, John Warwick ed., *Evidence for Faith: Deciding the God Question* (Probe, 1991)

Orr, James, *The Resurrection of Jesus* (Wipf & Stock Reprints, 2001)

* Parton, Craig, *Richard Whately: A Man For All Seasons* (Canadian Institute for Law, Theology & Public Policy, 1997), esp. the appendix, "Historic Doubts Relative to Napoleon Buonaparte"

* Rosenbladt, Rod, "The Integrity of the Gospel Writers" in Montgomery, John Warwick ed., *Christianity for the Tough Minded* (Canadian Institute for Law, Theology & Public Policy, 1973, 2001)

Smith, Wilbur M., *Therefore Stand* (W.A. Wilde, 1945)

Tolkien, J.R.R., "On Fairy Stories" in Lewis, C.S., *Essays Presented to Charles Williams* (Oxford University Press, 1947)

Wenham, John, *Easter Enigma* (Paternoster, 1984)

Wright, N.T., *The Challenge of Jesus* (Inter-Varsity Press, 1999)

## Legal Evidence

Dr. John Warwick Montgomery

* Montgomery, John Warwick, *Christ As Centre and Circumference* (Verlag fuer Kultur und Wissenschaft, 2012)

* Montgomery, John Warwick, *Christ Our Advocate* (Verlag fuer Kultur und Wissenschaft, 2002)

* Montgomery, John Warwick, *Human Rights and Human Dignity* (New Reformation Publications, 1986, 1995, 2015)

* Montgomery, John Warwick ed., *Jurisprudence: A Book of Readings* (New Reformation Publications, 1992, 2015)

* Montgomery, John Warwick, *The Law Above the Law* (New Reformation Publications, 1975, 2015)

* Montgomery, John Warwick, *Law and Christian Theology: Some Foundational Principles* (New Reformation Publications, 1996, 2013) [audio download]

* Montgomery, John Warwick, *Law and Gospel: A Study Integrating Faith and Practice* (New Reformation Publications, 1994, 2015)

* Montgomery, John Warwick, *Law and Morality: Friends or Foes?* (New Reformation Publications, 1994) Includes PDF of program. [audio and PDF download]

* Montgomery, John Warwick, *A Lawyer's Case for Christianity* (Canadian Institute for Law, Theology & Public Policy, 1996) [audiotape]

### Other Writers

Anderson, J.N.D., *A Lawyer Among the Theologians* (Hodder & Stoughton, 1973)

* Clifford, Ross, *Leading Lawyers' Case for the Resurrection* (New Reformation Publications, 1996, 2015)

* Greenleaf, Simon, "The Testimony of the Evangelists" in Montgomery, John Warwick, *The Law Above the Law* (New Reformation Publications, 1975, 2015)

## Evidence in General

*Global Journal of Classical Theology*, Vol. 3, No. 1 (2002) [www .globaljournalct.com]